In a Weekend: Lap Throws for the Family

Designs by Lisa Gentry

Waves of Gray, *page 8*

We're excited to bring you this great collection of throws that can each be made in a weekend! Designer Lisa Gentry put together designs that are just right for adults, teens and kids. Strategies like working with chunky-weight yarn or holding two strands of worsted-weight yarn together make the process faster. The repeats are easy to memorize so you don't have to consult your pattern every few rows. So, settle in with your favorite movies and crochet the weekend away. The lucky recipients of your crocheted wonders will be glad you did!

Table of Contents

General Information

Jewel Tone, *page 36*

Pretty Petals

Skill Level

INTERMEDIATE

Finished Measurements

35 inches wide x 45 inches long

Materials

- Caron Simply Soft medium (worsted) weight acrylic yarn (6 oz/315 yds/170g per skein): 6 skeins #9722 plum wine
- Size L/11/8mm crochet hook or size needed to obtain gauge
- Tapestry needle

4 MEDIUM

Gauge

With 2 strands held tog: 9 dc = 4 inches; 6 rows = 4 inches

Pattern Notes

Refer to Stitch Diagram as needed.

Hold 2 strands together unless otherwise stated.

Chain-3 at beginning of row counts as first double crochet unless otherwise stated.

Join with slip stitch as indicated unless otherwise stated.

Special Stitches

Circle: Fpdc *(see Stitch Guide)* around indicated st, ch 3, [fpdc around same st, ch 3] 4 times, turn work upside down, [fpdc around previous st, ch 3] 5 times, turn work right side up, fpdc around first st to complete circle.

Picot: (Sc, ch 3, sl st in 3rd ch from hook) as indicated in instructions.

Throw

Row 1 (RS): With 2 strands held tog *(see Pattern Notes)*, ch 83, dc in 4th ch from hook and in each rem ch across, turn. *(80 dc)*

Row 2 (WS): Ch 3 *(see Pattern Notes)*, dc in next dc and in each rem dc across, turn.

Rows 3–6: Rep row 2.

Row 7: Ch 3, dc in each of next 7 dc, **circle** *(see Special Stitches)* in next dc, [dc in dc behind previous circle, dc in each of next 15 dc, circle in next dc] 4 times, dc in dc behind previous circle, dc in each rem dc across, turn. *(5 circles)*

Row 8: Ch 3, dc in each of next 7 dc, sk next circle, [dc in each of next 16 dc, sk next circle] 4 times, dc in each rem dc across, turn.

Rows 9–12: Rep row 2.

Row 13: Ch 3, dc in each of next 15 dc, circle in next dc, [dc in dc behind previous circle, dc in each of next 15 dc, circle in next dc] 3 times, dc in dc behind previous circle, dc in each rem dc across, turn. *(4 circles)*

Row 14: Ch 3, dc in each of next 15 dc, sk next circle, [dc in each of next 16 dc, sk next circle] 3 times, dc in each rem dc across, turn.

Rows 15 & 16: Rep row 2.

Next rows: [Rep rows 3–16] 3 times.

Last rows: Rep rows 3–11. At end of last row, do not fasten off.

Border

Rnd 1 (RS): Ch 1, ***picot** *(see Special Stitches)* in each dc across long side, 2 picots in corner, [picot in next

dc, sk next dc] across short side, 2 picot in corner, rep from * around, **join** *(see Pattern Notes)* in first sc. Fasten off.

Finishing

Weave in ends. Block lightly to measurements if desired. ●

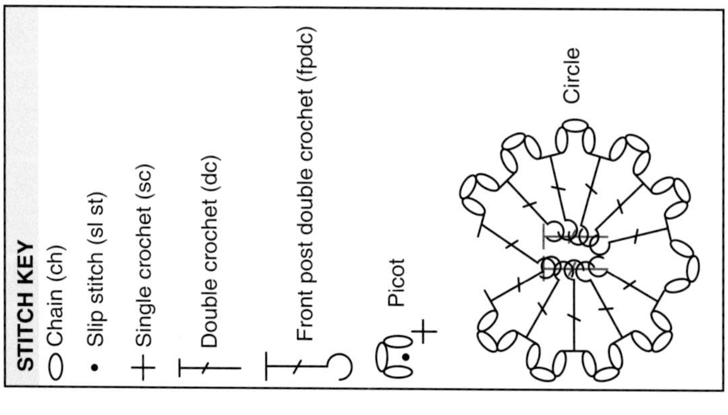

Misty Morning

Skill Level

INTERMEDIATE

Finished Measurements

38 inches wide x 47 inches long

Materials

- Caron One Pound medium (worsted) weight acrylic yarn (16 oz/812 yds/454g per skein):
  2 skeins #0617 medium grey mix
- Size J/10/6mm crochet hook or size needed to obtain gauge
- Tapestry needle

4 MEDIUM

Gauge

1 pattern rep = 4 inches; 6 rows = 3¾ inches

Pattern Notes

Refer to Stitch Diagram as needed.

Chain-3 at beginning of row counts as first double crochet unless otherwise stated.

Join with slip stitch as indicated unless otherwise stated.

Special Stitch

V-stitch (V-st): (Dc, ch 1, dc) in st as indicated in instructions.

Throw

Row 1 (RS): Ch 123, dc in 4th ch from hook and in each rem ch across, turn. *(120 dc)*

Row 2: Ch 3 *(see Pattern Notes)*, dc in next dc and in each rem st across, turn.

Row 3: Ch 3, dc in next dc, sk next dc, **V-st** *(see Special Stitch)* in next dc, sk next dc, [**fpdc** *(see Stitch Guide)* around each of next 3 dc, sk next dc, {V-st in next dc, sk next dc} 3 times] 9 times, fpdc around each of next 3 dc, sk next dc, V-st in next dc, sk next dc, dc in last 2 dc, turn. *(29 V-sts, 30 fpdc)*

Row 4: Ch 3, dc in next dc, V-st in ch-1 sp of next V-st, [**bpdc** *(see Stitch Guide)* around each of next 3 fpdc, V-st in ch-1 sp of each of next 3 V-sts] 9 times, bpdc around each of next 3 fpdc, V-st in ch-1 sp on next V-st, dc in last 2 dc, turn.

Row 5: Ch 3, dc in next dc, V-st in ch-1 sp of next V-st, [fpdc around each of next 3 bpdc, V-st in ch-1 sp of each of next 3 V-sts] 9 times, fpdc around each of next 3 bpdc, V-st in ch-1 sp on next V-st, dc in last 2 dc, turn.

Rows 6 & 7: Rep rows 4 and 5.

Row 8: Ch 3, dc in each of next 4 sts, [bpdc around each of next 3 fpdc, dc in each of next 9 sts] 9 times, bpdc around each of next 3 fpdc, dc in each of next 5 sts, turn.

Next rows: [Rep rows 3–8 consecutively] 11 times.

Last row: Ch 3, dc in each st across. Do not fasten off.

Border

Rnd 1: Ch 1, sc in each st and 2 sc in each row end around Throw, working 3 sc in each corner, **join** *(see Pattern Notes)* in first sc. Fasten off.

Finishing

Weave in ends. Block lightly to measurements if desired.

STITCH KEY

- Chain (ch)
- Slip stitch (sl st)
- Single crochet (sc)
- Double crochet (dc)
- Front post double crochet (fpdc)
- Back post double crochet (bpdc)
- V-stitch (V-st)
- Direction of work

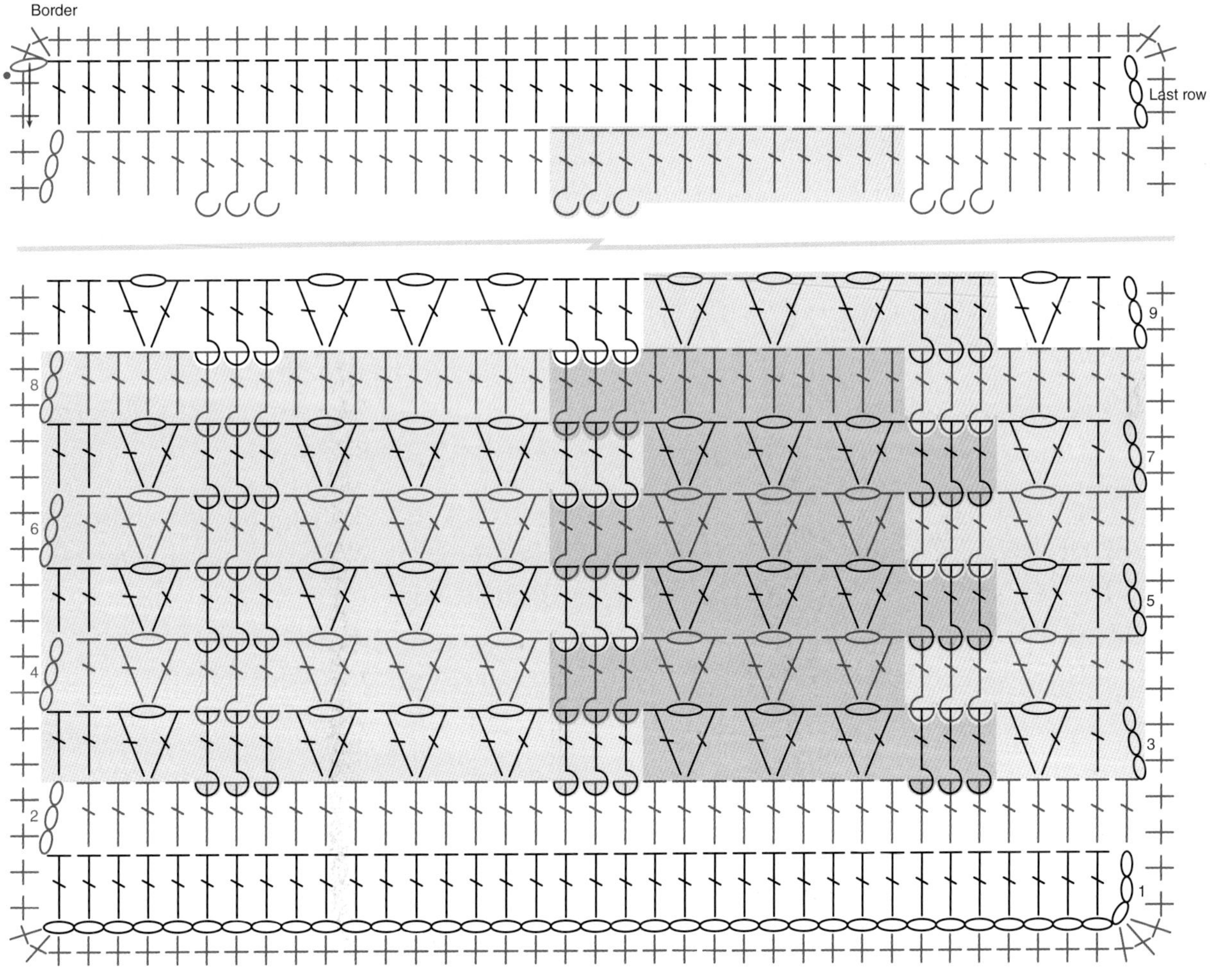

Misty Morning
Reduced Sample of Stitch Diagram
Note: *Reps shown in gray.*

Waves of Gray

Skill Level

EASY

Finished Measurements

36 inches wide x 44 inches long, with border

Materials

- Berroco Comfort Chunky bulky (chunky) weight nylon/acrylic yarn (3½ oz/150 yds/100g per skein):
  - 5 skeins #5703 barley
  - 6 skeins #5771 driftwood heather
- Size L/11/8mm crochet hook or size needed to obtain gauge
- Tapestry needle

5 BULKY

Gauge

1 pattern rep = 3¼ inches; 4 pattern rows = 2 inches

Pattern Notes

Refer to Stitch Diagram as needed.

When changing color, carry old color along side of work until next needed; do not fasten off old color unless otherwise stated.

Chain-3 at beginning of row counts as first double crochet unless otherwise stated.

Join with slip stitch as indicated unless otherwise stated.

Throw

Row 1 (WS): With barley, ch 102, sc in 2nd ch from hook and in each rem ch across, turn. *(101 sc)*

Row 2 (RS): Ch 1, sc in each sc across, **changing color** *(see Stitch Guide and Pattern Notes)* to driftwood in last st, turn.

Row 3: Ch 1, sc in each of first 2 sc, hdc in next sc, dc in each of next 5 sc, hdc in next sc, sc in next sc, *ch 1, sk next sc, sc in next sc, hdc in next sc, dc in each of next 5 sc, hdc in next sc, sc in next sc, rep from * across to last sc, sc in last sc, turn.

Row 4: Ch 1, sc in each of first 2 sc, hdc in next hdc, dc in each of next 5 dc, hdc in next hdc, sc in next sc, *ch 1, sk next ch-1 sp, sc in next sc, hdc in next hdc, dc in each of next 5 dc, hdc in next hdc, sc in next sc, rep from * across to last sc, sc in last sc, changing color to barley, turn.

Row 5: Ch 1, sc in each of first 10 sts, *working over ch-1 sps of previous 2 rows, dc in skipped sc on 3rd row below, sc in each of next 9 sts, rep from * across to last sc, sc in last sc, turn.

Row 6: Ch 1, sc in each st across, changing color to driftwood in last st, turn.

Row 7: Ch 3 *(see Pattern Notes)*, dc in each of next 2 sc, hdc in next sc, sc in next sc, ch 1, sk next sc, sc in next sc, hdc in next sc, *dc in each of next 5 sc, hdc in next sc, sc in next sc, ch 1, sk next sc, sc in next sc, hdc in next sc, rep from * across to last 3 sc, dc in each of last 3 sc, turn.

Row 8: Ch 3, dc in each of next 2 dc, hdc in next hdc, sc in next sc, ch 1, sk next ch-1 sp, sc in next sc, hdc in next hdc, *dc in each of next 5 dc, hdc in next hdc, sc in next sc, ch 1, sk next ch-1 sp, sc in next sc, hdc in next hdc, rep from * across to last 3 sts, dc in each of next 2 dc, dc in top of beg ch-3, changing color to barley in last st, turn.

Row 9: Ch 3, sc in each of first 5 sts, working over ch-1 sps of previous 2 rows, dc in sk sc on 3rd row below, *sc in each of next 9 sts, working over ch-1 sps of previous 2 rows, dc in sk sc on 3rd row below, rep from * across to last 5 sts, sc in each of next 4 sts, sc in top of beg ch-3, turn.

Row 10: Ch 1, sc in each st across, changing color to driftwood in last st, turn.

Next rows: [Rep rows 3–10] 11 times using the following color sequence: 2 rows driftwood, 2 rows barley, 2 rows driftwood, 1 row barley, 1 row driftwood, [2 rows barley, 2 rows driftwood] 16 times, 2 rows barley, 1 row driftwood, 1 row barley, [2 rows driftwood, 2 rows barley] 3 times.

Last rows: Rep rows 3–6 using the following color sequence: 2 rows driftwood, 2 rows barley. At end of last row, fasten off barley.

Border

Rnd 1 (WS): With driftwood, ch 1, [working across short side, sc in first sc, hdc in next sc, dc in next sc, tr in each of next 5 sc, dc in next sc, hdc in next sc, *sc in next sc, hdc in next sc, dc in next sc, tr in each of next 5 sc, dc in next sc, hdc in next sc, rep from * across to last sc, 2 sc in last sc, ch 4 *(corner made)*, working across long side, sc in next sc row, sk next sc row, **sc in next sc row, sk next sc row, hdc in next sc row, dc in next sc row, work 5 tr over next 2 dc rows, dc in next sc row, hdc in next sc row, rep from ** across to last 2 sc rows, sk next sc row, sc in next sc

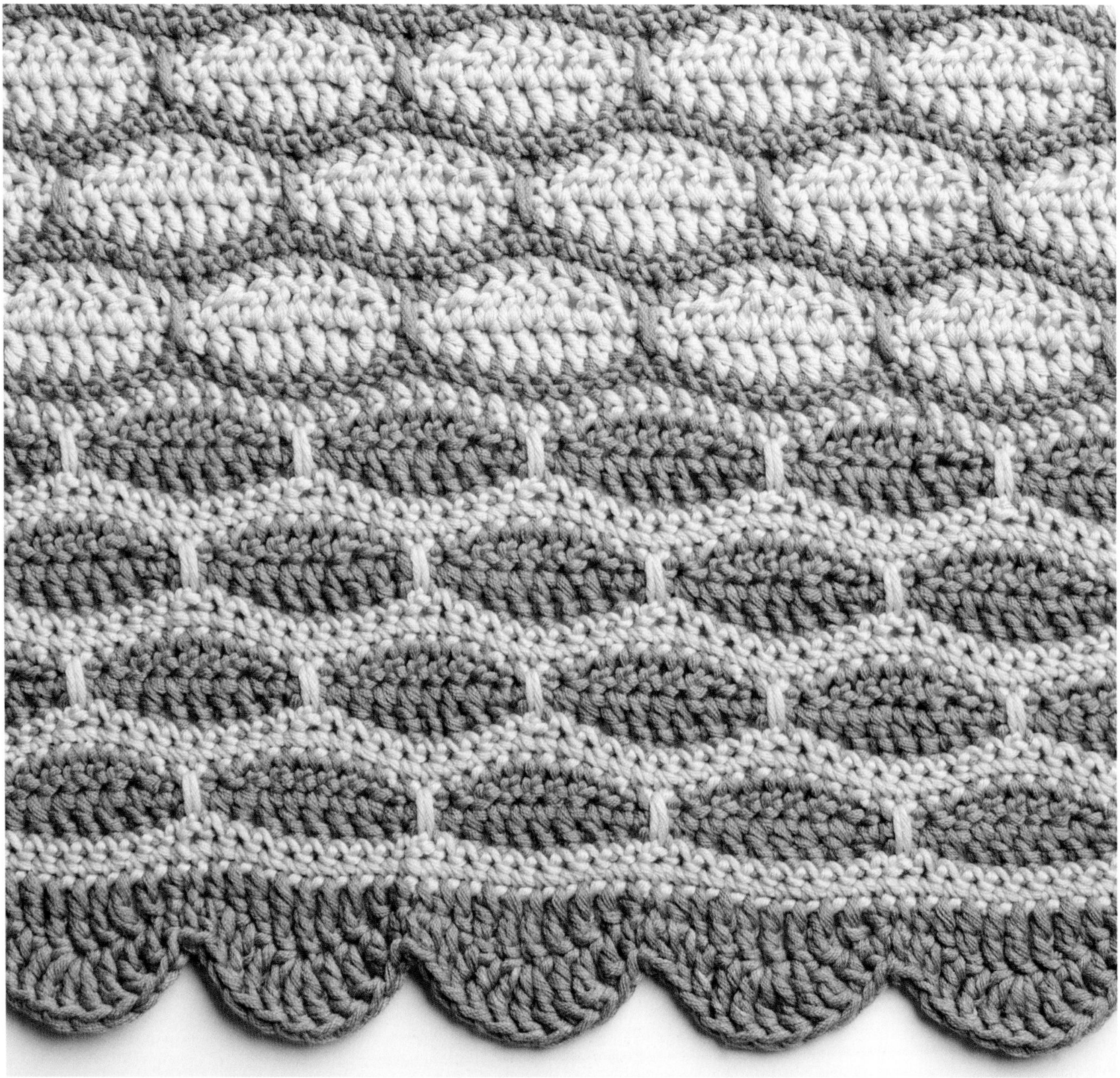

row, ch 4 *(corner made)*] twice, **join** *(see Pattern Notes)* in first sc.

Rnd 2: Ch 1, [sc in each of next 2 sc, *hdc in next hdc, dc in next dc, tr in each of next 2 tr, 3 tr in next tr, tr in each of next 2 tr, dc in next dc, hdc in next hdc, sc in next sc, rep from * across to last sc, sc in last sc, (hdc, dc, 3 tr, dc, hdc) in ch-4 corner sp] 4 times, join in first sc. Fasten off.

Finishing

Weave in ends. Block lightly to measurements if desired. ●

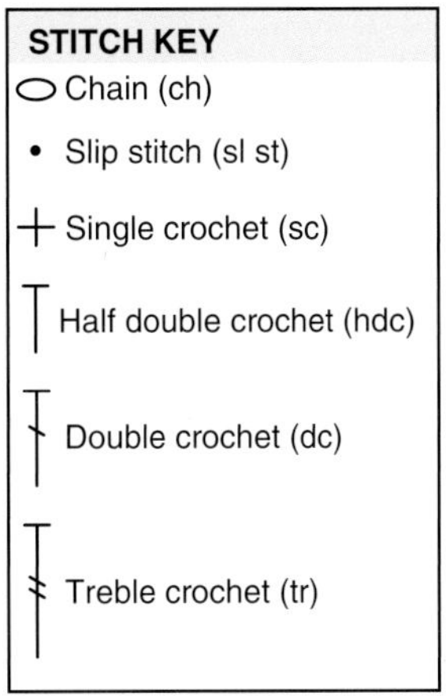

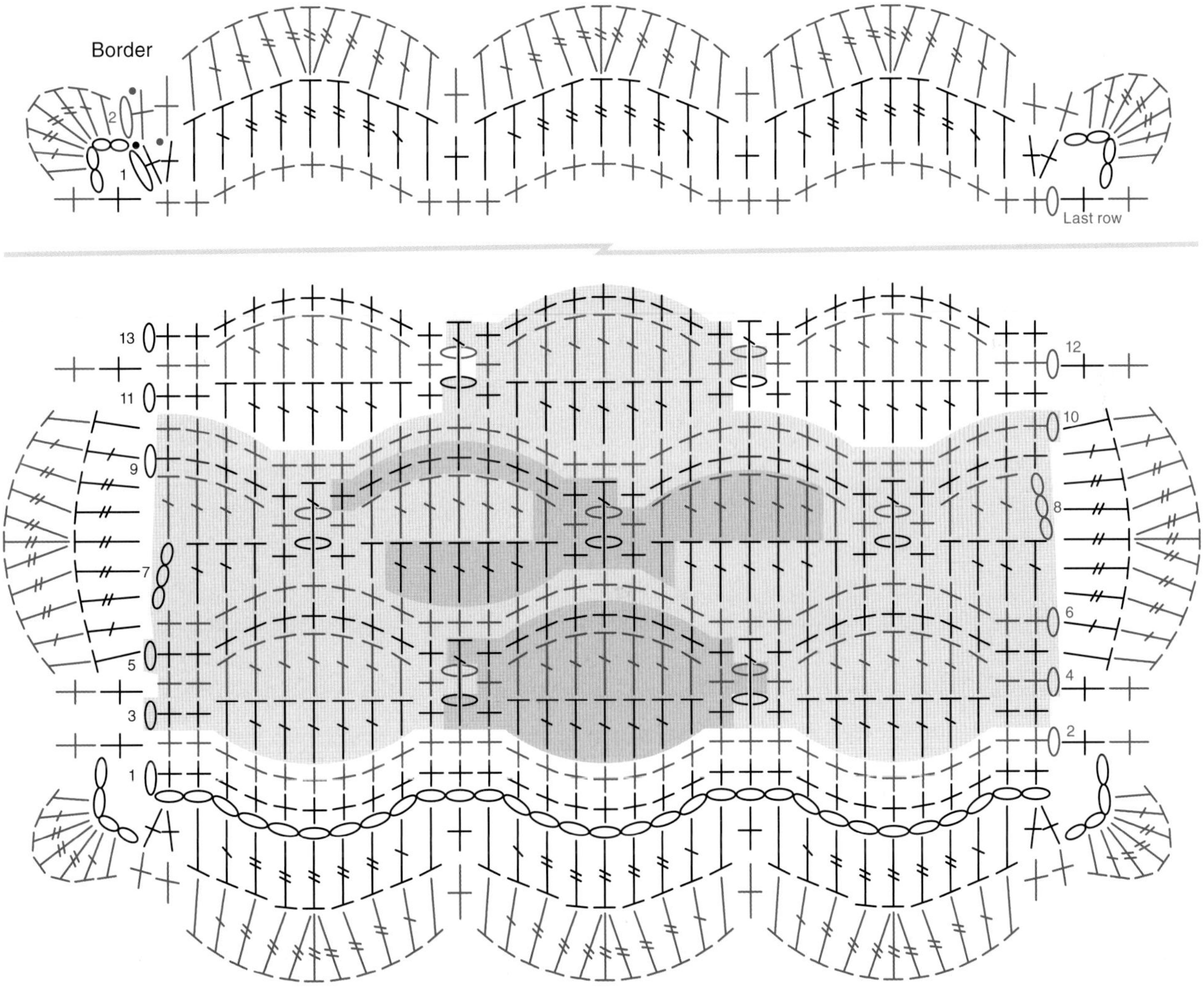

Waves of Gray
Reduced Sample of Stitch Diagram
***Note:** Reps shown in gray.*

Fall Foliage

Skill Level

INTERMEDIATE

Finished Measurements

36 inches wide x 47 inches long

Materials

- Plymouth Yarn Encore Chunky Colorspun bulky (chunky) weight acrylic/wool yarn (3½ oz/ 143 yds/100g per skein):
  - 9 skeins #7172 orange/gray/yellow variegated
- Sizes J/10/6mm and L/11/8mm crochet hooks or size needed to obtain gauge
- Tapestry needle

5 BULKY

Gauge

Size L hook: 3 pattern reps = 4 inches; 7 rows = 4 inches

Pattern Notes

Refer to Stitch Diagram as needed.

Chain-3 at beginning of row counts as first double crochet unless otherwise stated.

Join with slip stitch as indicated unless otherwise stated.

Special Stitch

V-stitch (V-st): (Dc, ch 1, dc) in st as indicated in instructions.

Throw

Row 1 (WS): With size L hook, ch 115, **V-st** *(see Special Stitch)* in 5th ch from hook, sk next ch, dc in next ch, *sk next ch, V-st in next ch, sk next ch, dc in next ch, rep from * across, turn. *(28 V-sts, 28 dc)*

Row 2 (RS): Ch 3 *(see Pattern Notes)*, *V-st in ch-1 sp of next V-st, **fpdc** *(see Stitch Guide)* around next dc, rep from * across to last V-st, V-st in ch-1 sp of next V-st, dc in top of beg ch-5, turn.

Row 3: Ch 3, *V-st in ch-1 sp of next V-st, dc in next fpdc, rep from * across to last V-st, V-st in ch-1 sp of last V-st, dc in top of beg ch-3, turn.

Row 4: Ch 3, *V-st in ch-1 sp of next V-st, fpdc around next dc, rep from * across to last V-st, V-st in ch-1 sp of next V-st, dc in top of beg ch-3, turn.

Rep rows 3 and 4 alternately until piece measures 46 inches or desired length, ending with WS row. Do not fasten off.

Edging

Rnd 1 (RS): With size J hook and working across last row, ch 3, work 3 dc in first dc *(corner made)*, 3 dc in ch-1 sp of next V-st, [sk next dc, fpdc around next dc, 3 dc in ch-1 sp of next V-st] across, 4 dc in top of beg ch-3 *(corner made)*, working across long side, 2 dc in each row end across, working across opposite side of foundation ch, 4 dc in first ch *(corner made)*, sk next ch, 3 dc in next ch, [sk next ch, fpdc around next dc on row 1, sk next ch, 3 dc in next ch] across, sk next ch, 4 dc in last ch *(corner made)*, working across 2nd long side, 2 dc in each row end across, **join** *(see Pattern Notes)* in top of beg ch-3. Fasten off.

Finishing

Weave in ends. Block lightly to measurements if desired. ●

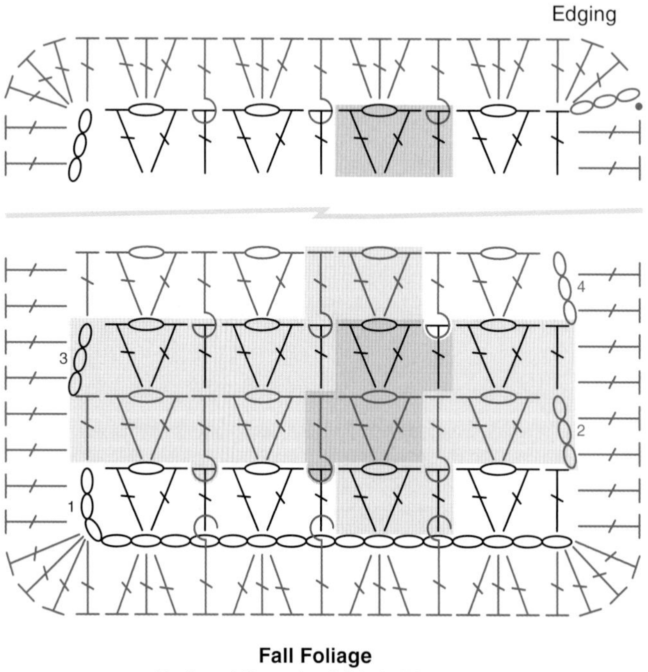

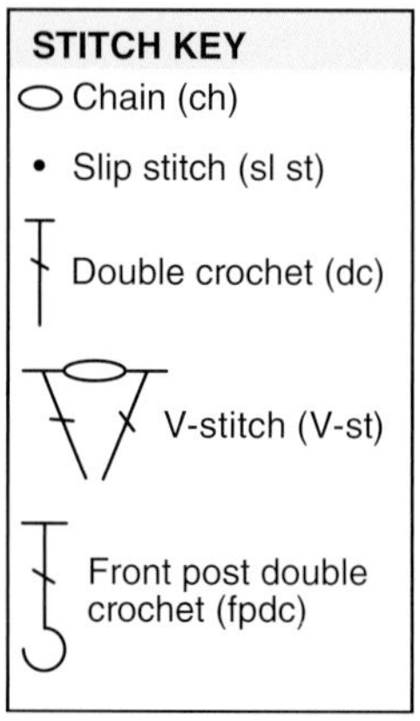

Fall Foliage
Reduced Sample of Stitch Diagram
Note: *Reps shown in gray.*

Fireside Classic

Skill Level

INTERMEDIATE

Finished Measurements

37 inches wide x 48 inches long

Materials

- Plymouth Yarn Encore Chunky bulky (chunky) weight acrylic/wool yarn (3½ oz/143 yds/100g per skein):
  8 skeins #1446 green/brown variegated
- Size L/11/8mm crochet hook or size needed to obtain gauge
- Tapestry needle

5 BULKY

Gauge

1 pattern rep = 3 inches; 4 pattern rows = 3 inches

Pattern Notes

Refer to Stitch Diagram as needed.

Chain-3 at beginning of row counts as first double crochet unless otherwise stated.

Join with slip stitch as indicated unless otherwise stated.

Special Stitches

Large puff (lg puff): [Yo, draw up lp in indicated st] 5 times, yo, draw through all lps on hook, push puff to RS.

Small puff (sm puff): [Yo, draw up lp in indicated st] 3 times, yo, draw through all lps on hook, push puff to RS.

Throw

Row 1 (RS): Ch 109, dc in 4th ch from hook and in each rem ch across, turn. *(107 dc)*

Row 2: Ch 3 *(see Pattern Notes)*, dc in next dc and in each rem st across, turn.

Row 3: Ch 3, dc in each of next 2 dc, [ch 2, sk next 2 dc, dc in next dc, {ch 1, sk next dc, dc in next dc} 3 times] 11 times, ch 2, sk next 2 dc, dc in last 3 dc, turn. *(50 dc, 12 ch-2 sps, 33 ch-1 sps)*

Row 4: Ch 3, dc in each of next 2 dc, [ch 2, sk next ch-2 sp, dc in next dc, {dc in next ch-1 sp, dc in next dc} 3 times] 11 times, ch 2, sk next ch-2 sp, dc in last 3 dc, turn. *(83 dc, 12 ch-2 sps)*

Row 5: Ch 3, dc in each of next 2 dc, ch 2, [sk next ch-2 sp, sk next dc, 2 dc in next dc, ch 1, sk next dc, **lg puff** *(see Special Stitches)* in next dc, ch 1, sk next dc, 2 dc in next dc, ch 2, sk next dc] 11 times, dc in last 3 dc, turn. *(50 dc, 12 ch-2 sps, 22 ch-1 sps, 11 lg puffs)*

Row 6: Ch 3, dc in each of next 2 sts, [ch 2, sk next ch-2 sp, dc in each of next 7 sts] 11 times, ch 2, sk next ch-2 sp, dc in each of last 3 sts, turn. *(83 dc, 12 ch-2 sps)*

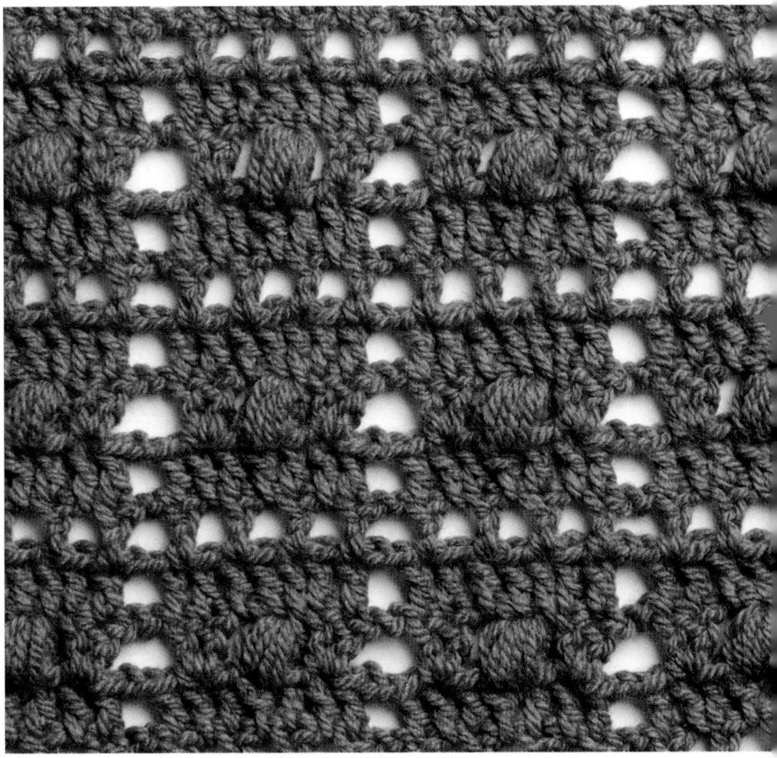

Row 7: Ch 3, dc in each of next 2 sts, [ch 2, sk next ch-2 sp, dc in next dc, {ch 1, sk next dc, dc in next dc} 3 times] 11 times, ch 2, sk next ch-2 sp, dc in each of last 3 sts, turn. *(50 dc, 12 ch-2 sps, 33 ch-1 sps)*

Rep rows 4–7 until piece measures 47 inches, ending with row 7.

Next row: Ch 3, dc in each st across, turn.

Last row: Ch 3, dc in each st across, do not turn. Do not fasten off.

Border

Rnd 1 (RS): With RS facing, ch 1, [working across long side, sk first dc, (sc, ch 2, **sm puff**—*see Special Stitches,* ch 2) in next dc *(corner made)*, *(sc, ch 2) in next dc, (sm puff, ch 2) in next dc, rep from * across to last row end, sk last row end, working across short edge, (sc, ch 2, sm puff, ch 2) in first dc *(corner made)*, **(sc, ch 2) in next dc, sk next dc, (sm puff, ch 2) in next dc, sk next dc, rep from ** across] twice, **join** *(see Pattern Notes)* in first sc. Fasten off.

Finishing

Weave in ends. Block lightly to measurements if desired. ●

STITCH KEY

- Chain (ch)
- Slip stitch (sl st)
- Single crochet (sc)
- Double crochet (dc)
- Large puff stitch (lg puff)
- Small puff stitch (sm puff)

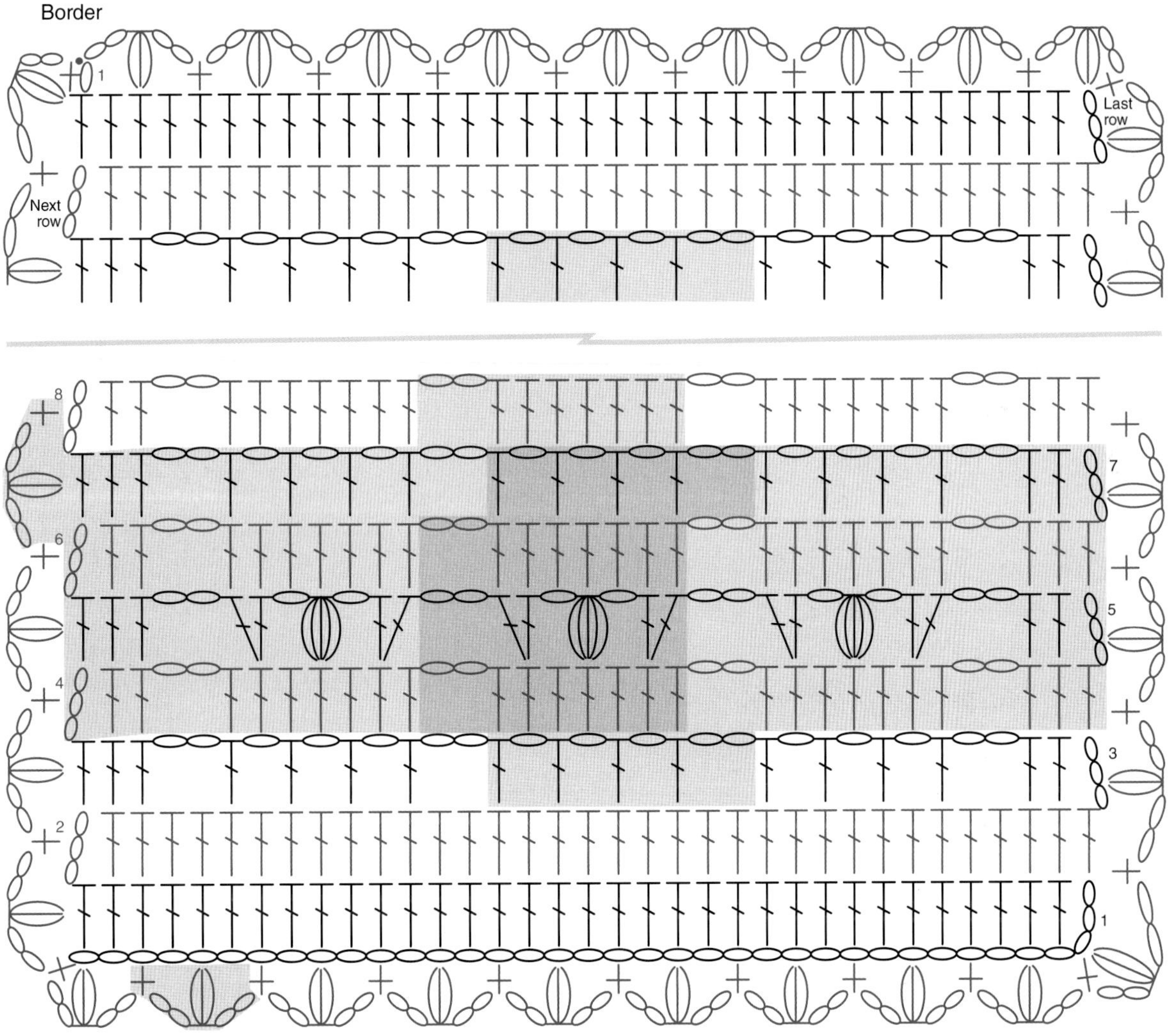

Stormy Night
Reduced Sample of Stitch Diagram
***Note:** Reps shown in gray.*

Hearts Galore

Skill Level

INTERMEDIATE

Finished Measurements

37 inches wide x 48 inches long

Materials

- Caron Simply Soft medium (worsted) weight acrylic yarn (6 oz/315 yds/170g per skein):
  - 4 skeins each #9604 watermelon and #9701 white
- Size L/11/8mm crochet hook or size needed to obtain gauge
- Tapestry needle

4 MEDIUM

Gauge

With 2 strands held tog: 2 pattern reps = 4 inches; 7 pattern rows = 4 inches

Pattern Notes

Refer to Stitch Diagram as needed.

Hold 2 strands together unless otherwise stated.

When changing color, carry old color along side of work until next needed; do not fasten off old color unless otherwise stated.

Chain-3 at beginning of row counts as first double crochet unless otherwise stated.

Join with slip stitch as indicated unless otherwise stated.

Special Stitches

Shell: 5 dc in indicated st.

Crossed V-stitch (cross V-st): Sk next sc, sc between sk sc and next dc, ch 1, sc between sk sc and previous dc.

Row end slip knot: Enlarge lp on hook, pull yarn through lp and pull to knot. Do not fasten off.

Beginning corner shell (beg corner shell): Ch 3, (dc, ch 3, 2 dc) as indicated in instructions.

Corner shell: (2 dc, ch 3, 2 dc) as indicated in instructions.

V-stitch (V-st): (2 dc, ch 1, 2 dc) as indicated in instructions.

Throw

Row 1 (RS): With 2 strands watermelon held tog *(see Pattern Notes)*, ch 94, 3 dc in 4th ch from hook *(sk ch-3 counts as first dc)*, sk next 2 chs, sc in next ch, *sk next 2 chs, **shell** *(see Special Stitches)* in next ch, sk next 2 chs, sc in next ch, rep from * across to last 4 chs, sk next 2 chs, 3 dc in next ch, dc in last ch, **changing color** *(see Stitch Guide and Pattern Notes)* to white in last st, turn. *(14 shells, 8 dc, 15 sc)*

Row 2 (WS): Ch 1, sc in each of first 2 dc, ch 1, **cross V-st** *(see Special Stitches)* over next st, ch 1, *sc in center dc of next shell, ch 1, cross V-st over next st, ch 1, rep from * across to last 4 dc, sk next 2 dc, sc in each of last 2 dc, **row end slip knot** *(see Special Stitches)*, do not turn. *(15 cross V-sts, 18 sc, 30 ch-1 sps)*

Row 3 (WS): With WS facing and watermelon, sl st in first sc, ch 1, sc in first sc, *sc in next sc, shell in center ch-1 sp of next cross V-st, rep from * across to last 2 sc, sc in each of last 2 sc, turn.

Row 4 (RS): With white, **ch 3** *(see Pattern Notes)*, 2 dc in next sc, ch 1, sc in center dc of next shell, ch 1, *cross V-st over next sc, ch 1, sc in center dc of next shell, ch 1, rep from * across to last 2 sc, 2 dc in next sc, dc in last sc, row end slip knot, do not turn. *(14 cross V-sts, 15 sc, 30 ch-1 sps).*

Row 5 (RS): With RS facing and watermelon sl st in first dc, ch 3, 3 dc in next dc, sk next dc, *sc in next

sc, shell in center ch-1 sp of next cross V-st, rep from * across to last 3 dc, sk next dc, 3 dc in next dc, dc in last dc, turn. *(14 shells, 15 sc, 8 dc)*

Rep rows 2–5 until piece measures 40 inches from beg, ending with row 5 (RS). Fasten off white.

Border

Row 1: Working across long side with watermelon, 120 sc evenly sp across. Fasten off.

Row 2: Working across opposite long side with RS facing, **join** *(see Pattern Notes)* watermelon in first row end, ch 1, 120 sc evenly sp across. Fasten off.

Rnd 1: Now working in rnds, join white in first dc in right top corner, **beg corner shell** *(see Special Stitches)* in first dc, dc in each of next 3 dc, sk next sc, [dc in each of next 5 dc, sk next sc] 14 times, dc in each of next 3 dc, **corner shell** *(see Special Stitches)* in last dc, working across long side, dc in each sc, working across opposite side of foundation ch, corner shell in first ch, dc in each of next 3 chs, sk next ch, [dc in each of next 5 chs, sk next ch] 14 times, dc in each of next 3 chs, corner shell in last ch, working across opposite long side, dc in each sc across, join in top of beg ch-3. Fasten off white. *(352 dc, 4 corner shells)*

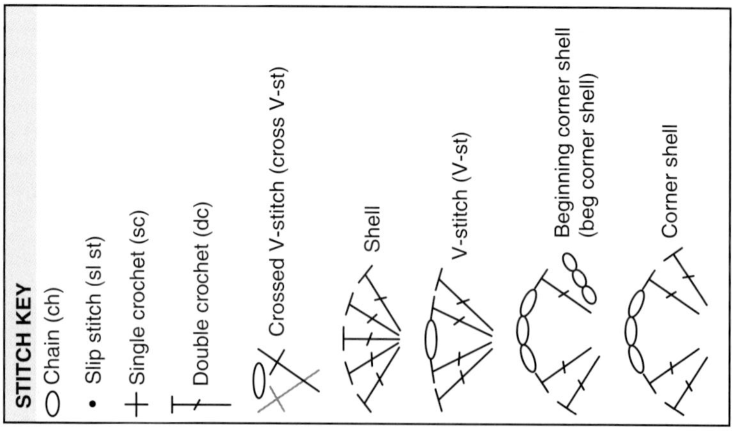

Rnd 2: Join watermelon in right top corner ch-3 sp, beg corner shell in same corner ch-3 sp, *working across short side, ch 3, sk first 8 dc, **V-st** *(see Special Stitches)* in next dc, [ch 3, sk next 6 dc, V-st in next dc] 9 times, ch 3, sk next 8 dc, corner shell in next corner ch-3 sp, working across long side, ch 3, sk first 6 dc, V-st in next dc, ch 3, sk next 6 dc] 14 times**, corner shell in next corner ch-3 sp, rep from * once, ending last rep at **, join in top of beg ch-3. Fasten off watermelon.

Rnd 3: Join white in right top corner ch-3 sp, beg corner shell in same corner ch-3 sp, *ch 2, working over ch-3 sp, sk next 2 dc on rnd 1, dc in each of next 2 dc on rnd 1, ch 2, *sc in next ch-1 sp, ch 2, sk next 2 dc on rnd 1, dc in each of next 2 dc on rnd 1, ch 2, rep from * across to corner ch-3 sp**, corner shell in corner ch-3 sp, rep from * around, ending last rep at **, join in top of beg ch-3.

Rnd 4: Sl st in next dc, sl st in next corner ch-3 sp, beg corner shell in same corner ch-3 sp, dc in each dc and ch across to next corner ch-3 sp, corner shell in corner ch-3 sp, rep from * around, ending last rep at **, join in top of beg ch-3. Fasten off.

Finishing

Weave in ends. Block lightly to measurements if desired. ●

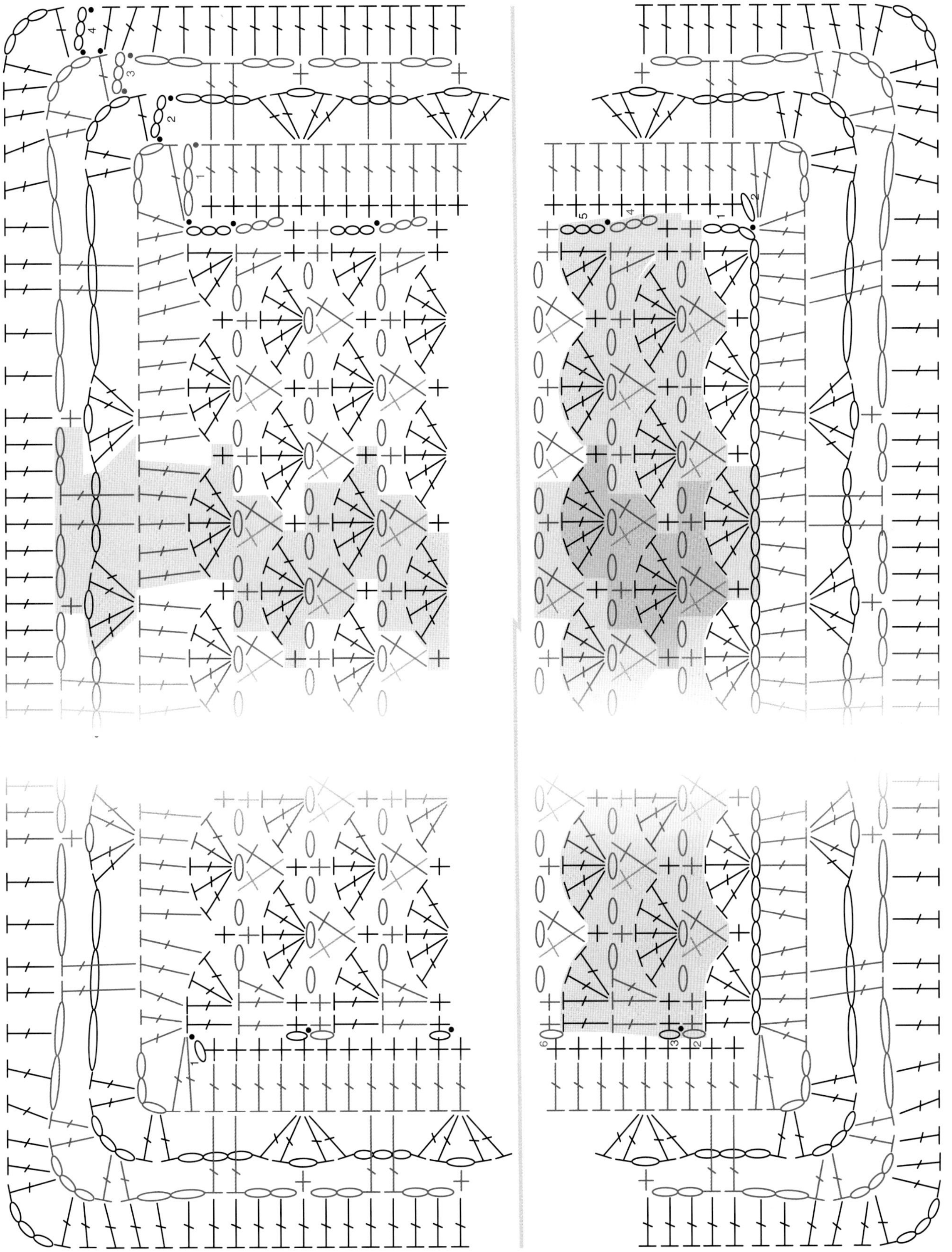

Hearts Galore
Reduced Sample of Stitch Diagram
Note: *Reps shown in gray.*

Camo Commando

Skill Level

EASY

Finished Measurements

35 inches wide x 48 inches long

Materials

- Caron Simply Soft Camo medium (worsted) weight acrylic yarn (4 oz/204 yds/113g per skein):
  10 skeins #11483 renegade camo
- Size L/11/8mm crochet hook or size needed to obtain gauge
- Tapestry needle

4 MEDIUM

Gauge

With 2 strands held tog: 1 pattern rep = 3½ inches; 7 rows = 4 inches

Pattern Notes

Refer to Stitch Diagram as needed.

Hold 2 strands together unless otherwise stated.

Chain-3 at beginning of row counts as first double crochet unless otherwise stated.

Join with slip stitch as indicated unless otherwise stated.

Special Stitches

Beginning corner shell (beg corner shell): Ch 3, (dc, ch 1, 2 dc, ch 1, 2 dc) as indicated in instructions.

Shell: (2 dc, ch 1, 2 dc) as indicated in instructions.

Corner shell: (2 dc, ch 1, 2 dc, ch 1, 2 dc) as indicated in instructions.

Throw

Row 1 (RS): With 2 strands held tog *(see Pattern Notes)*, ch 125, 2 dc in 3rd ch from hook, *ch 4, sk next 3 chs, sc in next ch, ch 3, sk next 2 chs, sc in next ch, ch 4, sk next 3 chs, 3 dc in next ch, rep from * across, turn. *(12 3-dc groups)*

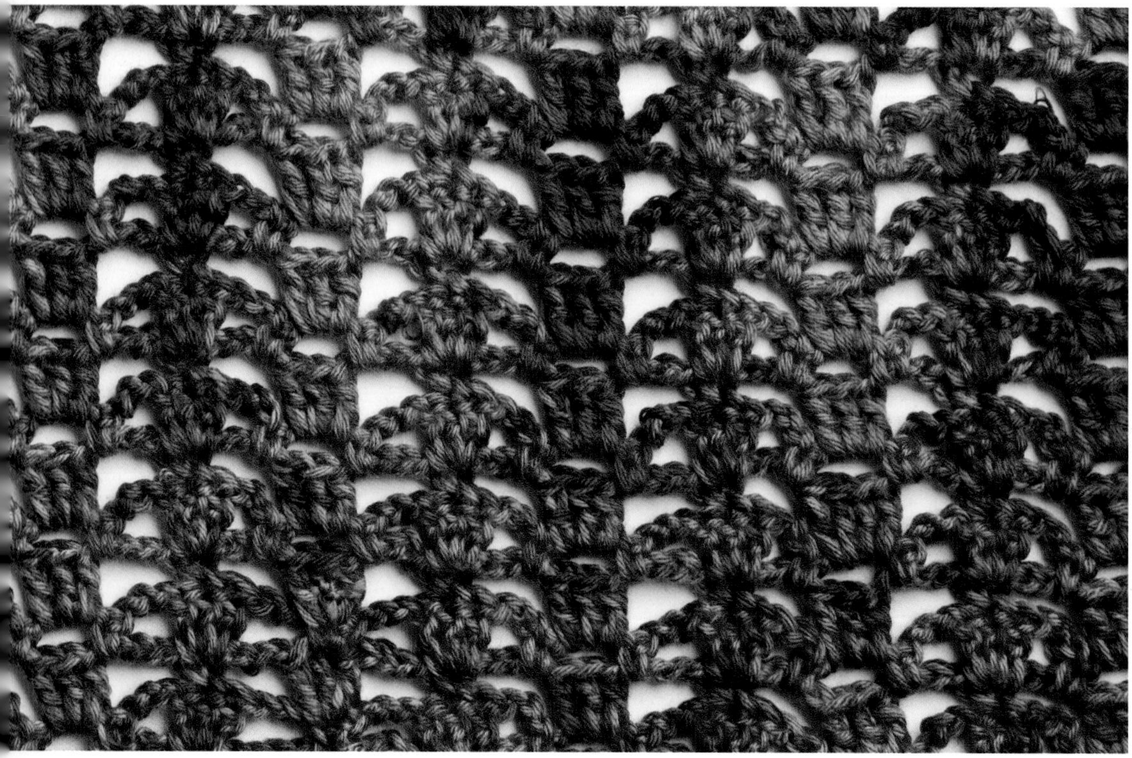

Row 2 (WS): Ch 1, sc in first dc, *ch 5, 3 dc in next ch-3 sp, ch 5, sc in center dc of next 3-dc group, rep from * across, working last sc in top of beg ch-2, turn.

Row 3: Ch 3 *(see Pattern Notes)*, 2 dc in first sc, *ch 4, sc in next ch-5 sp, ch 3, sc in next ch-5 sp, ch 4, 3 dc in next sc, rep from * across, turn.

Row 4: Ch 1, sc in first dc, *ch 5, 3 dc in next ch-3 sp, ch 5, sc in center dc of next 3-dc group, rep from * across, working last sc in top of beg ch-3, turn.

Rep rows 3 and 4 until piece measures 46 inches or desired length, ending with RS row. Do not fasten off.

Border

Rnd 1: Beg corner shell *(see Special Stitches)* in first dc, ch 1, **shell** *(see Special Stitches)* in next ch-3 sp, [ch 1, shell in center dc of next 3-dc group, ch 1, shell in next ch-3 sp] across, **corner shell** *(see Special Stitches)* in last dc, working across long side, 4 dc in each sc across, working across opposite side of foundation ch, corner shell in first foundation ch, sk next 4 chs, shell in next ch-2 sp, [sk next 4 chs, shell in next ch, sk next 4 chs, shell in next ch-2 sp] across to last 5 chs, sk next 4 chs, corner shell in last ch, working across opposite long side, 4 dc in each sc across, **join** *(see Pattern Notes)* in top of beg ch-3. Fasten off.

Finishing

Weave in ends. Block lightly to measurements if desired. ●

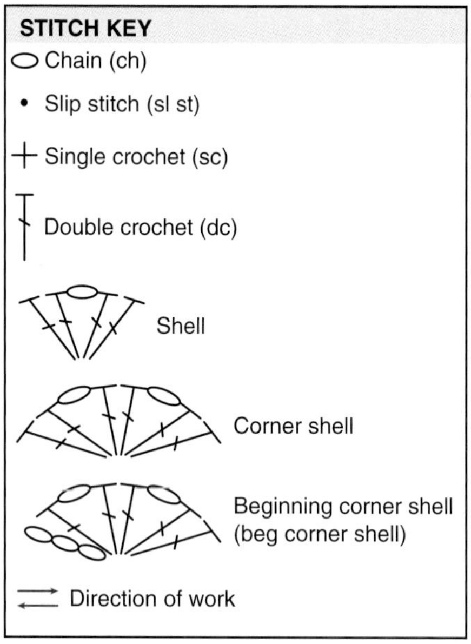

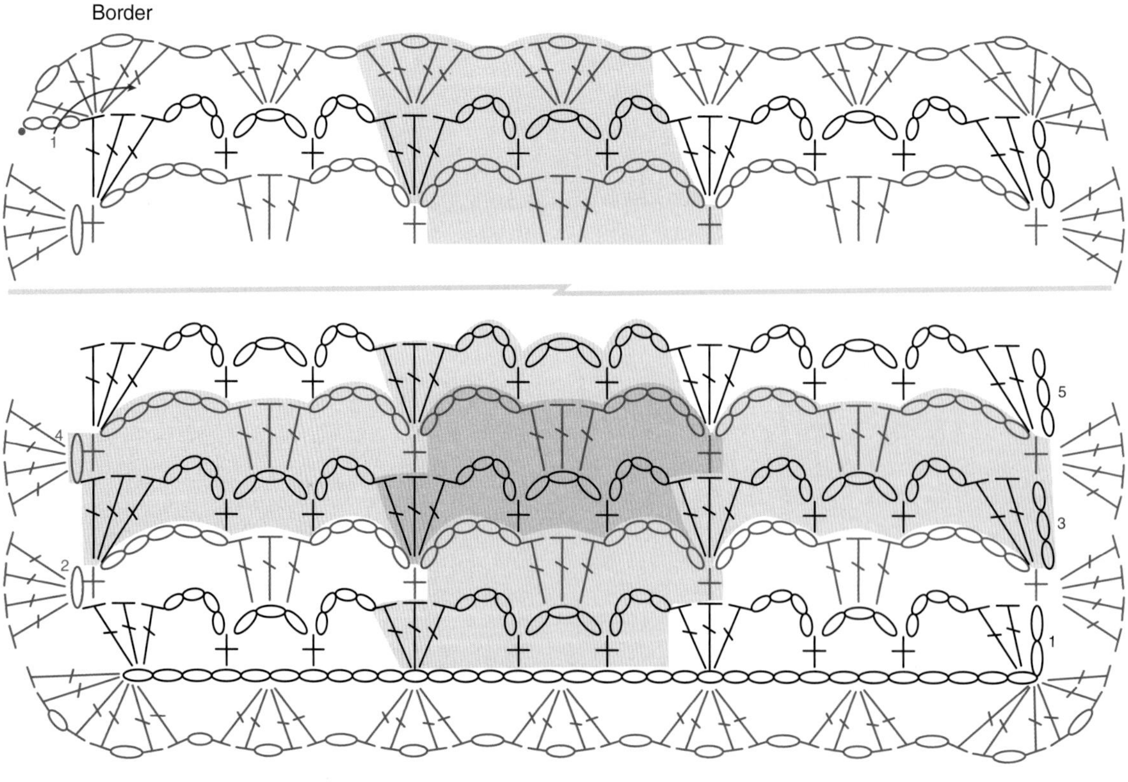

Camo Commando
Reduced Sample of Stitch Diagram
Note: *Reps shown in gray.*

Sweet & Sassy

Skill Level

INTERMEDIATE

Finished Measurements

35 inches wide x 45 inches long

Materials

- Premier Yarns Deborah Norville Everyday Soft Worsted medium (worsted) weight acrylic yarn (solids: 4 oz/203 yds/113g; multis: 3½ oz/180 yds/100g per skein):
  3 skeins each #2008 parfait and #1012 black
- Size K/10½/6.5mm crochet hook or size needed to obtain gauge
- Tapestry needle

Gauge

2 pattern reps = 3¼ inches; 9 pattern rows = 4¼ inches

Pattern Notes

Refer to Stitch Diagram as needed.

When changing color, carry old color along side of work until next needed; do not fasten off unless otherwise stated.

Chain-3 at beginning of row counts as first double crochet unless otherwise stated.

Join with slip stitch as indicated unless otherwise stated.

Special Stitches

Shell: 3 dc as indicated in instructions.

V-stitch (V-st): (Dc, ch 1, dc) as indicated in instructions.

Row end slip knot: Enlarge lp on hook, pull yarn through lp and pull to knot. Do not fasten off.

Beginning corner shell (beg corner shell): Ch 3, (dc, ch 2, 2 dc) as indicated in instructions.

Corner shell: (2 dc, ch 2, 2 dc) as indicated in instructions.

Border shell: 4 dc as indicated in instructions.

Throw

Row 1 (RS): With parfait, ch 122, sc in 2nd ch from hook, *ch 1, sk next 2 chs, **shell** *(see Special Stitches)* in next ch, ch 1, sk next 2 chs, sc in next ch, rep from * across, **changing color** *(see Stitch Guide and Pattern Notes)* to black in last st, turn. *(20 shells)*

Row 2 (WS): With black, **ch 3** *(see Pattern Notes)*, dc in first sc, [ch 1, sc in center dc of next shell, ch 1, **V-st** *(see Special Stitches)* in next sc] 19 times, ch 1, sc in center dc of next shell, ch 1, 2 dc in last sc, **row end slip knot** *(see Special Stitches)*, do not turn. *(19 V-sts)*

Row 3 (WS): With parfait, ch 1, sc in first dc, [ch 1, shell in next sc, ch 1, sc in ch-1 sp of next V-st] 19 times, ch 1, shell in next sc, ch 1, sc in last dc, row end slip knot, turn.

Row 4 (RS): With black, ch 3, dc in first sc, *[ch 1, sc in center dc of next shell, ch 1, V-st in next sc] 19 times,

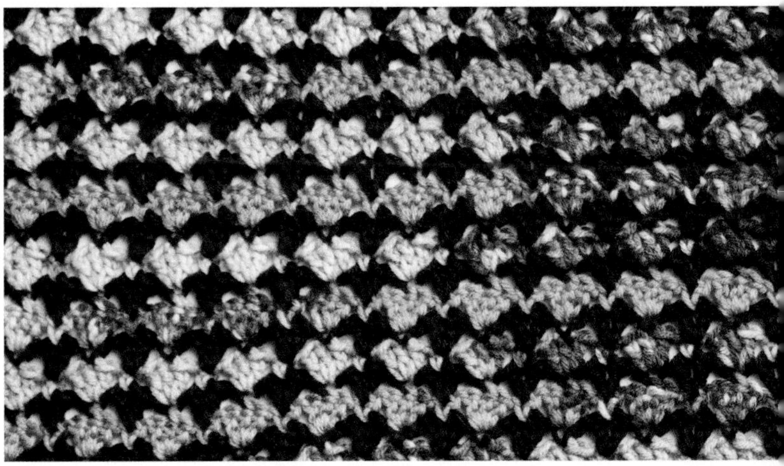

ch 1, sc in center dc of next shell, ch 1, 2 dc in last sc, row end slip knot, do not turn.

Row 5 (RS): With parfait, ch 1, sc in first dc, [ch 1, shell in next sc, ch 1, sc in ch-1 sp of next V-st] 19 times, ch 1, shell in next sc, ch 1, sc in last dc, row end slip knot, turn.

Rep rows 2–5 until piece measures 42 inches from beg, ending with row 3. Fasten off parfait.

Border

Rnd 1 (RS): With black, **beg corner shell** *(see Special Stitches)* in first sc in top right corner, [ch 2, sc in center dc of next shell, ch 2, V-st in next sc] 19 times, ch 2, sc in center dc of last shell, ch 2, **corner shell** *(see Special Stitches)* in last sc, working across long side, *ch 2, sc in first dc row end, ch 2, [V-st in next dc row end, ch 2, sc in next dc row end, ch 2] across*, working across opposite side of foundation ch, corner shell in first ch, [ch 2, sk next 2 chs, sc in next ch, ch 2, sk next 2 chs, V-st in next ch] 19 times, ch 2, sk next 2 chs, sc in next ch, ch 2, sk next 2 chs, corner shell in last ch, working across opposite long side, rep from * to *, **join** *(see Pattern Notes)* in top of beg ch-3. Fasten off black.

Rnd 2 (RS): Join parfait in next corner ch-2 sp, beg corner shell in same sp, *ch 1, **border shell** *(see Special Stitches)* in next sc, ch 1, [sc in next V-st, ch 1, border shell in next sc, ch 1] across**, corner shell in next ch-2 corner sp, rep from * 3 times, ending last rep at **, join in top of beg ch-3. Fasten off parfait.

Finishing

Weave in ends. Block lightly to measurements if desired. ●

Border

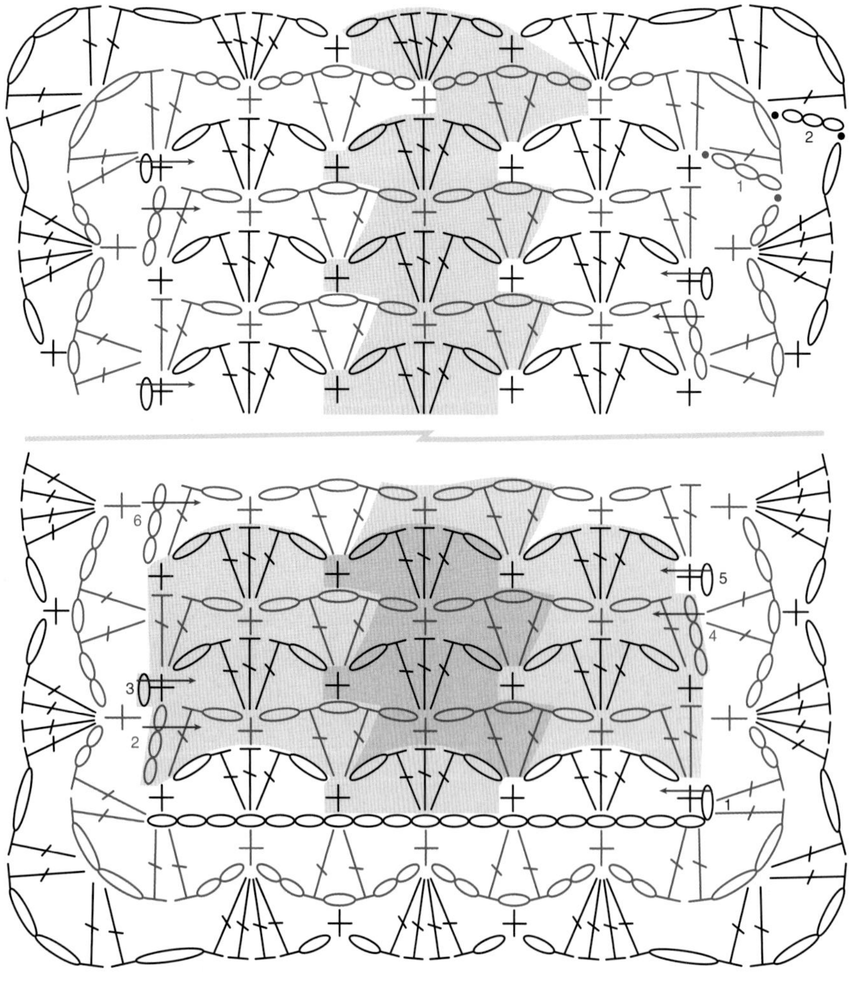

Sweet & Sassy
Reduced Sample of Stitch Diagram
Note: *Reps shown in gray.*

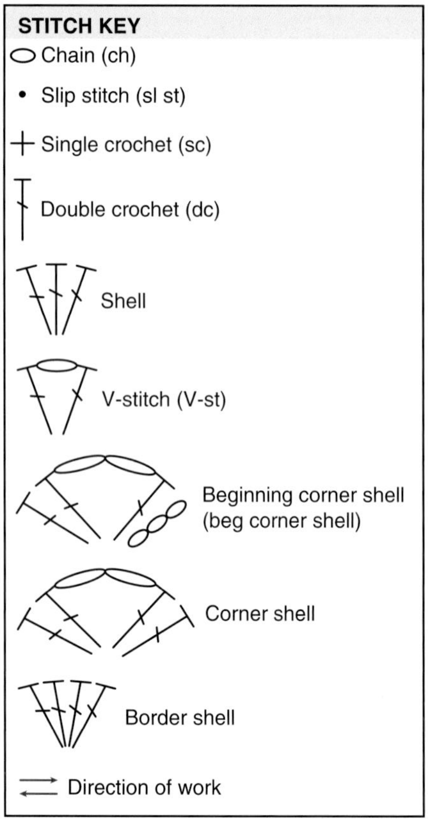

Calming Ripples

Skill Level

EASY

Finished Measurements

36 inches wide x 47 inches long

Materials

- Premier Yarns Deborah Norville Everyday Soft Worsted medium (worsted) weight acrylic yarn (4 oz/203 yds/113g per skein):
  4 skeins each #1017 azure, #1024 steel and #1030 glass
- Sizes I/9/5.5mm and L/11/8mm crochet hooks or size needed to obtain gauge
- Tapestry needle

4 MEDIUM

Gauge

With 2 strands held tog and size I hook: 1 pattern rep = 5½ inches; 8 rows = 4 inches

Pattern Notes

Refer to Stitch Diagram as needed.

Throw is worked with size L hook and 2 strands of yarn held together unless otherwise stated.

Chain-3 at beginning of row counts as first double crochet unless otherwise stated.

Chain spaces count as stitches.

Border is worked with 1 strand of yarn and size I hook unless otherwise stated.

Join with slip stitch as indicated unless otherwise stated.

Special Stitches

Double crochet decrease over 3 stitches (dc dec over 3): Yo, insert hook in first indicated st and pull up lp, yo and pull through 2 lps on hook, yo, sk next indicated st, insert hook in last indicated st and pull up lp, yo, pull through all lps on hook.

Small shell (sm shell): (Dc, ch 3, dc) as indicated in instructions.

Double crochet decrease over 5 stitches (dc dec over 5): Yo, insert hook in first indicated st and pull up lp, yo and pull through 2 lps on hook, yo, sk next 3 indicated sts, insert hook in last indicated st and pull up lp, yo, pull through all lps on hook.

Large shell (lg shell): (2 dc, ch 3, 2 dc) as indicated in instructions.

Cluster (cl): Ch 5, yo, insert hook in 5th ch from hook and draw up lp, yo and draw through 2 lps on hook, yo, insert hook in same ch and draw up lp, yo and draw through all lps on hook.

Throw

Row 1 (RS): With size L hook and 2 strands azure held tog *(see Pattern Notes)*, ch 107, dc in 4th ch from hook, **dc dec over 3** *(see Special Stitches)* in next 3 chs, *[ch 1, sk next ch, dc in next ch] 3 times, ch 1, sk next ch, **sm shell** *(see Special Stitches)* in next ch, [ch 1, sk 1 ch, dc in next ch] 3 times, ch 1, sk next ch**, **dc dec over 5** *(see Special Stitches)* in next 5 chs, rep from * 4 times, ending last rep at **, dc dec over 3 in next 3 chs, dc in last 2 chs, turn. *(6 sm shells)*

Row 2: Ch 3 *(see Pattern Notes)*, dc in next dc, dc dec over 3 in **next 3 sts** *(see Pattern Notes)*, [dc in next ch-1 sp, dc in next dc] 3 times, ***lg shell** *(see Special*

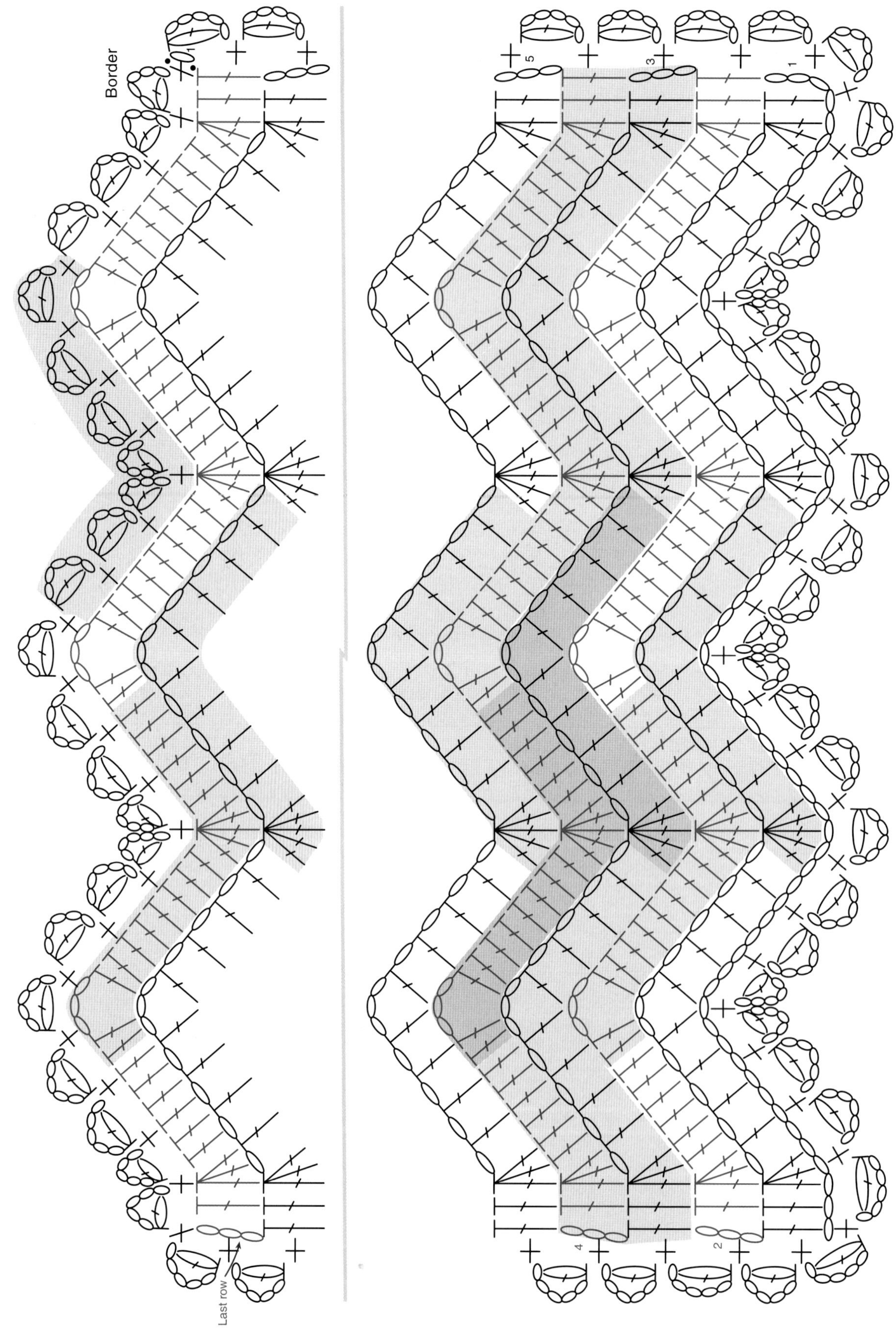

Calming Ripples
Reduced Sample of Stitch Diagram
Note: *Reps shown in gray.*

Stitches) in next ch-3 sp, [dc in next dc, dc in next ch-1 sp] 3 times**, dc dec over 5 in next 5 sts, rep from * 4 times, ending last rep at **, dc dec over 3 in next 3 sts, dc in next st, dc in top of beg ch-4, **changing color** *(see Stitch Guide)* to steel in last st, turn. Fasten off azure.

Row 3: Ch 3, dc in next dc, dc dec over 3 in next 3 sts, *[ch 1, sk next dc, dc in next ch] 3 times, ch 1, sm shell in next ch-3 sp, ch 1, [dc in next ch, ch 1, sk next st] 3 times**, dc dec over 5 in next 5 sts, rep from * 4 times, ending last rep at **, dc dec over 3 in next 3 sts, dc in next st, dc in top of beg ch-3, turn.

Row 4: Ch 3, dc in next dc, dc dec over 3 in next 3 sts, [dc in next ch-1 sp, dc in next dc] 3 times, *lg shell in next ch-3 sp, [dc in next dc, dc in next ch-1 sp] 3 times**, dc dec over 5 in next 5 sts, rep from * 4 times, ending last rep at **, dc dec over 3 in next 3 sts, dc in next st, dc in top of beg ch-3, changing color to glass in last st, turn. Fasten off steel.

Rows 5 & 6: With glass, rep rows 3 and 4, changing color to azure in last st of last row.

Rows 7 & 8: With azure, rep rows 3 and 4.

Rows 9–44: [Rep rows 3–8 consecutively] 6 times. At end of last row, fasten off.

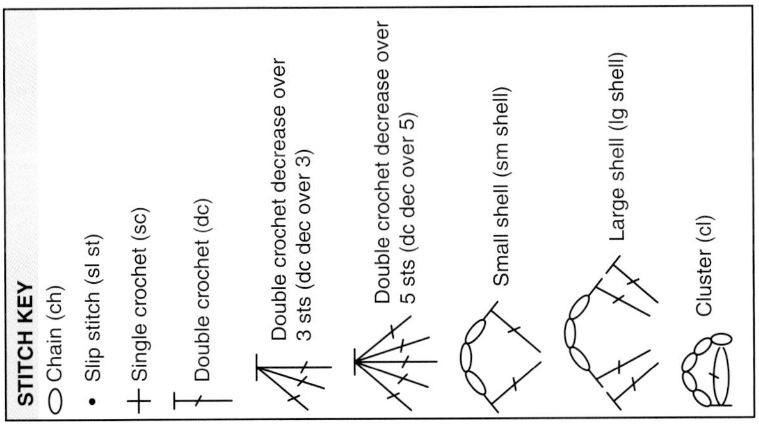

Border

Rnd 1: With RS facing and **size I hook and 1 strand of glass** *(see Pattern Notes)*, **join** *(see Pattern Notes)* glass in first dc, ch 1, (sc, **cl**—*see Special Stitches*) in same dc, sk next dc, [(sc, cl) in next dc, sk next 2 dc] 3 times, *([sc, cl] twice) in ch-3 sp of next lg shell**, [sk next 2 dc, (sc, cl) in next dc] 5 times, sk next 2 dc, rep from * across, ending last rep at **, [sk next 2 dc, (sc, cl) in next dc] 3 times, sk next dc, (sc, cl) in last st, working across long side, (sc, cl) in each row end across, working across opposite side of foundation ch, (sc, cl) in first ch, ***[sk next 2 chs, (sc, cl) in next ch] 6 times****, sk next 2 chs, (sc, cl) in next ch, sk next ch, (sc, cl) in next ch, rep from *** across, ending last rep at ****, sk next 2 chs, (sc, cl) in last ch, working across opposite long side, (sc, cl) in each row end across, join in beg ch-1. Fasten off.

Finishing

Weave in ends. Block lightly to measurements if desired. ●

Color Riot

Skill Level

INTERMEDIATE

Finished Measurements

35 inches wide x 45 inches long

Materials

- Caron Simply Soft medium (worsted) weight acrylic yarn (6 oz/315 yds/170g per skein):
  4 skeins each #9778 orange and #9711 dark country blue
- Sizes I/9/5.5mm and L/11/8mm crochet hooks or size needed to obtain gauge
- Tapestry needle

4 MEDIUM

Gauge

With 2 strands held tog and size L hook: 1 pattern rep = 2½ inches; 2 pattern rows = 2¾ inches

Pattern Notes

Refer to Stitch Diagram as needed.

Throw is worked with size L hook and 2 strands of yarn held together unless otherwise stated.

Chain-3 at beginning of row counts as first double crochet unless otherwise stated.

When changing color, carry old color along side of work until next needed; do not fasten off unless otherwise stated.

Border is worked with size I hook and 1 strand of yarn unless otherwise stated.

Join with slip stitch as indicated unless otherwise stated.

Special Stitches

Half shell: 4 dc as indicated in instructions.

Shell: 7 dc as indicated in instructions.

Double crochet decrease over 9 stitches (dc dec over 9): Holding back last lp of each st on hook, dc in same dc as last st made, in each of next 3 dc, in next st, and in each of next 4 dc, yo and draw through all 10 lps on hook, ch 1.

Beginning double crochet decrease over 5 stitches (beg dc dec over 5): Holding back last lp of each st on hook, dc in next sc and in each of next 4 dc, yo and draw through all 6 lps on hook, ch 1.

Double crochet decrease over 5 stitches (dc dec over 5): Holding last lp of each st on hook, dc in same sc as last dc made, in each of next 3 dc, and in next sc, yo and draw through all 6 lps on hook, ch 1.

Beginning corner shell (beg corner shell): Ch 3, (dc, ch 2, 2 dc) as indicated in instructions.

Corner shell: (2 dc, ch 2, 2 dc) as indicated in instructions.

Single crochet corner shell (sc corner shell): (2 sc, ch 2, 2 sc) as indicated in instructions.

Throw

Row 1 (RS): With **size L hook and 2 strands of orange held tog** *(see Pattern Notes)*, ch 101, sc in 2nd ch from hook and in each rem ch across, turn. *(100 sc)*

Row 2: Ch 3 *(see Pattern Notes)*, dc in next sc, **half shell** *(see Special Stitches)* in next sc, sk next 3 sc, sc in next sc, *sk next 3 sc, **shell** *(see Special Stitches)* in next sc, sk next 3 sc, sc in next sc, rep from * across to last 6 sc, sk next 3 sc, half shell in next sc, dc in each of next 2 sc, **changing color** *(see Stitch Guide and Pattern Notes)* to blue in last st, turn. *(11 shells, 2 half shells, 4 dc, 12 sc)*

Row 3: Ch 1, sc in each of first 3 dc, [ch 3, **dc dec over 9** *(see Special Stitches)* in same dc as last sc made and in next 8 sts, ch 3, sc in same st as last dc made] 12 times, sc in each of next 2 dc, turn. *(12 dc dec over 9, 17 sc, 24 ch-3 sps)*

Row 4: Ch 1, sc in each of first 3 sc, [shell in top of next dc dec over 9, sc in next sc] 12 times, sc in each of next 3 sc, changing color to orange in last st, turn. *(12 shells, 17 sc)*

Row 5: Ch 3, dc in next sc, **beg dc dec over 5** *(see Special Stitches)* in next sc and next 4 dc, ch 3, sc in same st as last dc made, [ch 3, dc dec over 9 in same dc as last sc made and in next 8 sts, ch 3, sc in same st as last dc made] 11 times, ch 3, **dc dec over 5** *(see Special Stitches)* in same st as last dc made, next 3 dc and next sc, dc in each of next 2 sc, turn. *(11 dc dec over 9, 2 dc dec over 5, 4 dc, 12 sc, 24 ch-3 sps)*

Row 6: Ch 3, dc in next sc, half shell in top of next dc dec over 5, sc in next sc, [shell in top of next dc dec over 9, sc in next sc] 11 times, 4 dc in top of next dc dec over 5, dc in each of next 2 dc, changing color to blue in last st, turn. *(11 shells, 2 half shells, 12 sc, 4 dc)*

Rows 7–50: [Rep rows 3–6 consecutively] 11 times.

Rows 51–53: Rep rows 3–5.

Row 54: Ch 1, sc in each of first 2 dc, sc in top of next dc dec over 5, sc in each of next 3 chs, sc in next sc, sc in each of next 3 chs, [sc in top of next dc dec over 9, sc in each of next 3 chs, sc in next sc, sc in each of next 3 chs] 11 times, sc in top of next beg dc dec over 5, sc in each of next 2 dc. Fasten off.

Border

Rnd 1 (RS): With **size I hook and 1 strand of blue** *(see Pattern Notes)*, **join** *(see Pattern Notes)* blue in first st of row 54, **beg corner shell** *(see Special Stitches)* in same st, *dc in each rem st across to last st, **corner shell** *(see Special Stitches)* in last st, working across long side, 2 dc in each dc row end and dc in each sc row end across, working across opposite side of foundation ch, corner shell in first ch, dc in each rem ch across to last ch, corner shell in last ch, working across opposite long side, 2 dc in each dc row end and dc in each sc row end across, join in top of beg ch-3.

Rnd 2: Sl st in next dc and in corner ch-2 sp, beg corner shell in same sp, *dc in each dc across to next corner**, corner shell in corner, rep from * around, ending last rep at **, join in top of beg ch-3. Fasten off blue.

Rnd 3: Join orange in next corner ch-2 sp, ch 1, ***sc corner shell** *(see Special Stitches)* in same corner ch-2 sp, sc in each dc across, rep from * around, join in first sc. Fasten off orange.

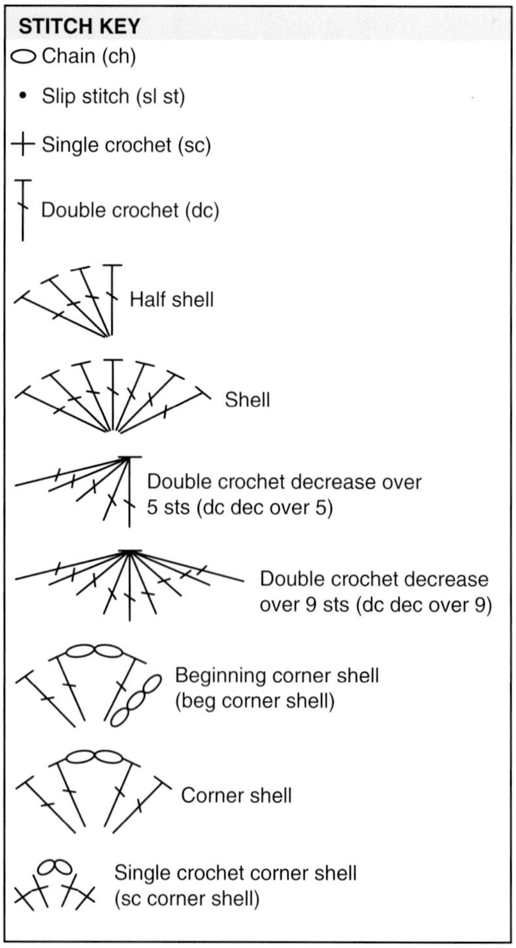

Rnd 4: Join blue in next corner ch-2 sp, beg corner shell in same corner ch-2 sp, *dc in each sc to across next corner ch-2 sp**, corner shell in corner ch-2 sp, rep from * around, ending last rep at **, join in top of beg ch-3. Fasten off blue.

Finishing

Weave in ends. Block lightly to measurements if desired. ●

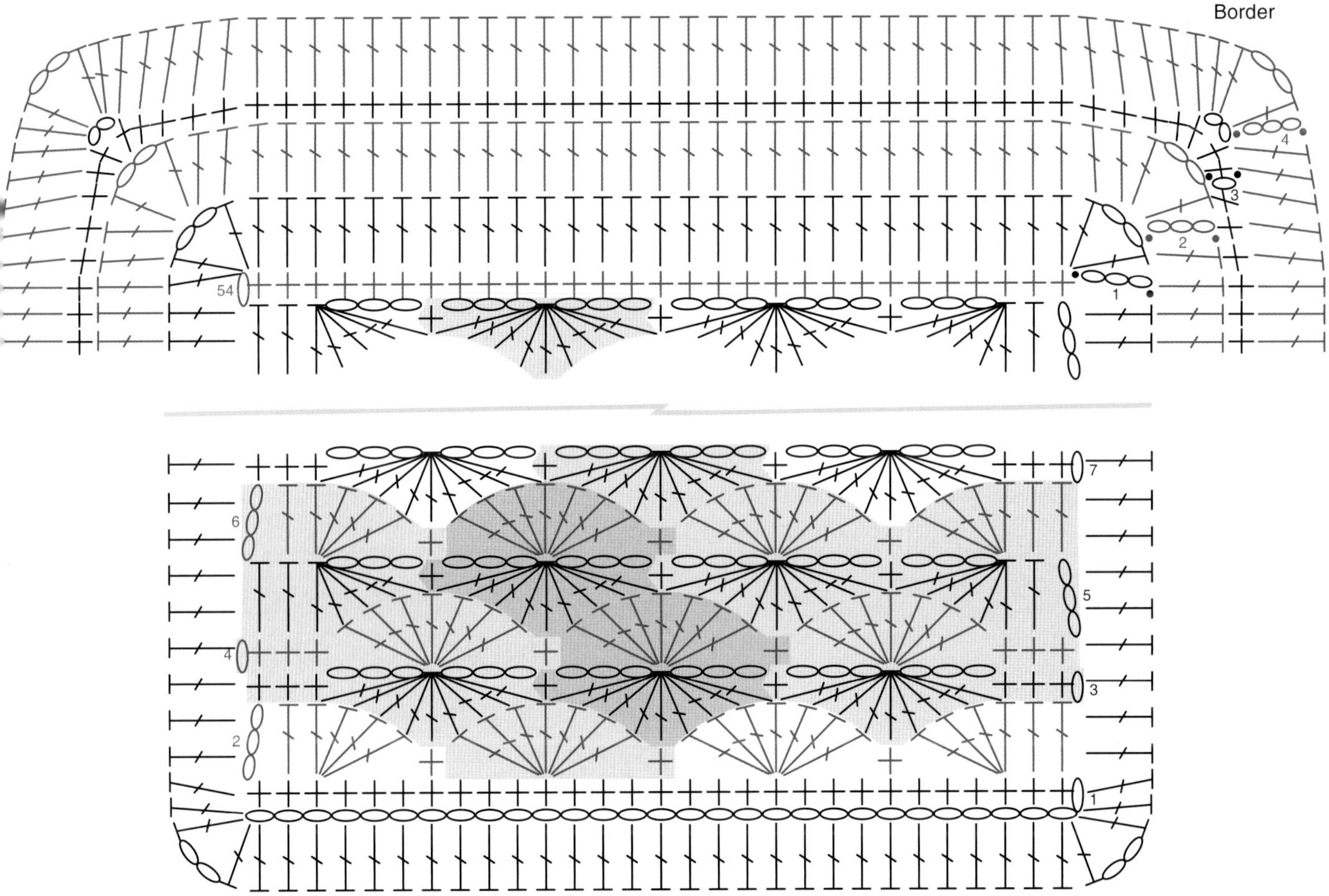

Color Riot
Reduced Sample of Stitch Diagram
Note: *Reps shown in gray.*

Jewel Tone

Skill Level

EASY

Finished Measurements

35 inches wide x 48 inches long

Materials

- Plymouth Yarn Encore Chunky Colorspun bulky (chunky) weight acrylic/wool yarn (3½ oz/ 143 yds/100g per skein):
  - 8 skeins #7129 blue/green/purple variegated
- Size K/10½/6.5mm crochet hook or size needed to obtain gauge
- Tapestry needle

5 BULKY

Gauge

12 dc = 4 inches; 6 dc rows = 4 inches

Pattern Notes

Refer to Stitch Diagram as needed.

Chain-3 at beginning of row counts as first double crochet unless otherwise stated.

Chain-5 at beginning of row counts as first double crochet and chain-2 space unless otherwise stated.

Chain-8 at beginning of row counts as first double crochet and chain-5 space unless otherwise stated.

Join with slip stitch as indicated unless otherwise stated.

Special Stitches

Beginning corner shell (beg corner shell): Ch 3, (dc, ch 2, 2 dc) as indicated in instructions.

Corner shell: (2 dc, ch 2, 2 dc) as indicated in instructions.

Shell: (Sc, ch 3, 2 dc) as indicated in instructions.

Throw

Row 1 (RS): Ch 103, dc in 3rd ch from hook and in each rem ch across, turn. *(101 dc)*

Row 2: Ch 3 *(see Pattern Notes)*, dc in next dc and in each rem dc across, turn.

Row 3: Ch 1, sc in each of first 2 dc, *ch 3, sk next dc, sc in each of next 3 dc, rep from * across to last 3 dc, ch 3, sk next dc, sc in each of next 2 dc, turn. *(25 ch-3 sps, 76 sc)*

Row 4: Ch 5 *(see Pattern Notes)*, sc in next ch-3 sp, *ch 5, sc in next ch-3 sp, rep from * across to last ch-3 sp, sc in last ch-3 sp, ch 2, dc in last sc, turn. *(24 ch-5 sps, 25 sc, 2 dc, 2 ch-2 sps)*

Row 5: Ch 1, sc in first dc, ch 5, sc in next ch-5 sp, [ch 2, dc in next sc, ch 2, sc in next ch-5 sp, ch 5, sc in next ch-5 sp] 11 times, ch 2, dc in next sc, ch 2, sc in next ch-5 sp, ch 5, sc in 3rd ch of beg ch-5, turn. *(13 ch-5 sps, 12 dc, 24 ch-2 sps, 26 sc)*

Row 6: Ch 5, [sc in next ch-5 sp, ch 3, 3 dc in next dc, ch 3, sc in next ch-5 sp] 12 times, ch 2, dc in last sc, turn. *(38 dc, 24 ch-3 sps, 2 ch-2 sps, 13 sc)*

Row 7: Ch 8 *(see Pattern Notes)*, [dc in next ch-3 sp, dc in each of next 3 dc, dc in next ch-3 sp, ch 5] 12 times, dc in 3rd ch of beg ch-5, turn. *(62 dc, 13 ch-5 sps)*

Row 8: Ch 5, [sc in next ch-5 sp, ch 3, sk next dc, dc in each of next 3 dc, ch 3] 12 times, sc in next ch-5 sp, dc in 3rd ch of beg ch-8, turn. *(38 dc, 24 ch-4 sps, 2 ch-2 sps, 13 sc)*

Row 9: Ch 1, sc in first dc, [ch 5, sc in next ch-3 sp, ch 3, sk next dc, dc in next dc, ch 3, sc in next ch-3 sp] 12 times, ch 5, sc in 3rd ch of beg ch-5, turn. *(13 ch-5 sps, 12 dc, 24 ch-3 sps, 26 sc)*

Row 10: Ch 5, sc in first ch-5 sp, [ch 3, sc in next dc, ch 3, sc in next ch-5 sp] 12 times, ch 2, dc in last sc, turn. *(24 ch-3 sps, 25 sc, 2 dc, 2 ch-2 sps)*

Row 11: Ch 3, dc in first ch-2 sp, *dc in next sc, 3 dc in next ch-3 sp, rep from * across to last sc, dc in last sc, dc in last ch-2 sp, dc in 3rd ch of beg ch-5, turn. *(101 dc)*

Rows 12–14: Ch 3, dc in next dc and in each rem dc across, turn.

Rows 15–74: [Rep rows 3–14 consecutively] 5 times.

Rows 75–84: Rep rows 3–12. At end of last row, do not fasten off.

Border

Rnd 1 (RS): Beg corner shell *(see Special Stitches)* in first dc, dc in each rem dc across to last dc, **corner shell** *(see Special Stitches)* in last dc, working across long side, *2 dc in each of next 2 dc row ends, 13 tr evenly sp in next 8 row ends, work 2 dc in each of next 2 dc row ends*, rep from * to * across, working across opposite side of foundation ch, corner shell in first ch, dc in each rem ch across to last ch, corner shell in last ch, working across opposite long side, rep from * to *, **join** *(see Pattern Notes)* in top of beg ch-3.

Rnd 2: Sl st in next dc, sl st in next ch-2 sp, beg corner shell in same sp, *[sk next 3 dc, **shell** *(see Special Stitches)* in next dc, sk next 3 dc] across to next corner**, sl st in corner ch-2 sp, beg corner shell in same sp, rep from * around, ending last rep at **, join in top of beg ch-3. Fasten off.

Finishing

Weave in ends. Block lightly to measurements if desired. ●

STITCH KEY

- Chain (ch)
- Slip stitch (sl st)
- Single crochet (sc)
- Double crochet (dc)
- Beginning corner shell (beg corner shell)
- Corner shell
- Shell

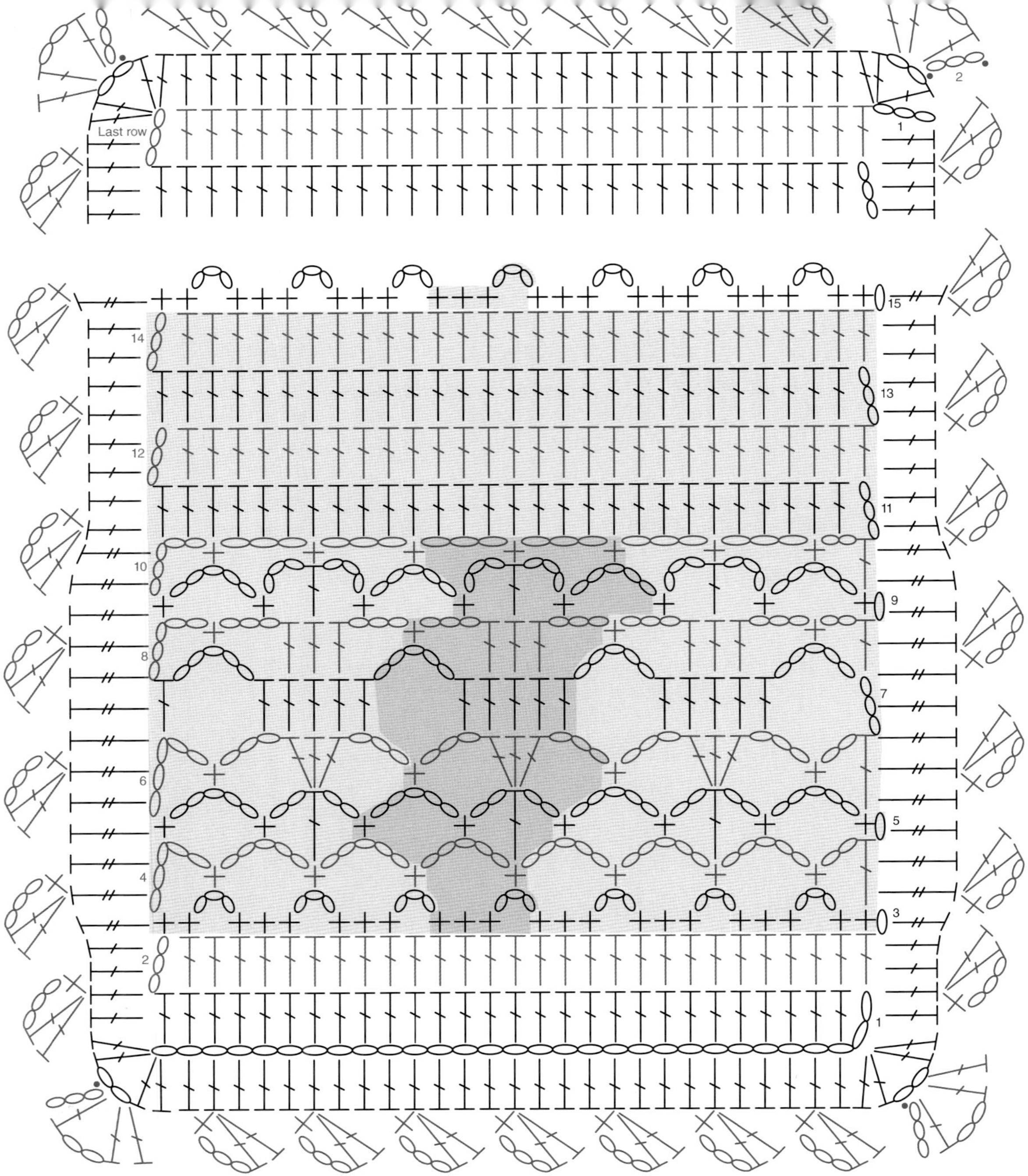

Jewel Tone
Reduced Sample of Stitch Diagram
Note: *Reps shown in gray.*

Watercolor Violets

Skill Level

EASY

Finished Measurements

35 inches wide x 45 inches long

Materials

- Premier Yarns Deborah Norville Everyday Soft Worsted medium (worsted) weight acrylic yarn (3½ oz/180 yds/100g per skein):
  6 skeins #2022 lilac ridge
- Size J/10/6mm crochet hook or size needed to obtain gauge
- Tapestry needle

4 MEDIUM

Gauge

2 pattern reps = 3½ inches; 5 rows = 4 inches

Pattern Notes

Refer to Stitch Diagram as needed.

Chain-4 at beginning of row counts as first treble crochet unless otherwise stated.

Chain-3 at beginning of row counts as first double crochet unless otherwise stated.

Join with slip stitch as indicated unless otherwise stated.

Special Stitches

V-stitch (V-st): (Dc, ch 1, dc) as indicated in instructions.

Shell: 5 tr as indicated in instructions.

Throw

Row 1 (WS): Ch 113, dc in 4th ch from hook, dc in next ch, *sk next ch, **V-st** *(see Special Stitches)* in next ch, sk next ch, dc in each of next 3 chs, rep from * across, turn. *(57 dc, 18 V-sts)*

Row 2 (RS): Ch 4 *(see Pattern Notes)*, tr in next dc, ***shell** *(see Special Stitches)* in ch-1 sp of next V-st, sk next dc, tr in next dc, rep from * across to last dc, tr in last dc, turn. *(21 tr, 18 shells)*

Row 3 (WS): Ch 3 *(see Pattern Notes)*, working in **front lp** *(see Stitch Guide)*, dc in each of next 2 tr, *sk next tr, V-st in next tr, sk next tr, dc in each of next 3 tr, rep from * across, turn. *(57 dc, 18 V-sts)*

Rep rows 2 and 3 alternately until piece measures 42 inches or desired length, ending with RS row. Fasten off.

Border

Row 1 (WS): With WS facing, **join** *(see Pattern Notes)* in first ch of foundation ch, ch 2 *(corner made)*, working across long side of Throw, dc in first dc, 2 dc in next tr, [V-st in next dc, 3 dc in next tr] across, ch 2 *(corner made)*, working across short row, dc in each of first 3 tr, [sk next tr, V-st in next tr, sk next tr, dc in each of next 3 tr] across, ch 2 *(corner made)*, working across opposite long side, dc in first dc, 2 dc in next tr, [V-st in next dc, 3 dc in next tr] across, ch 2 *(corner made)*, sl st in next foundation ch, turn.

Rnd 2 (RS): Ch 4, 6 tr in corner ch-2 sp, *sk next dc, sc in next dc, [shell in ch-1 sp of next V-st, sk next dc, sc in next dc] across to next corner, 7 tr in corner ch-2 sp, rep from * twice, sc in next ch, [sk next 2 chs, shell in next ch, sk next 2 chs, sc in next ch] across, join in top of beg ch-4. Fasten off.

Finishing

Weave in ends. Block lightly to measurements if desired. ●

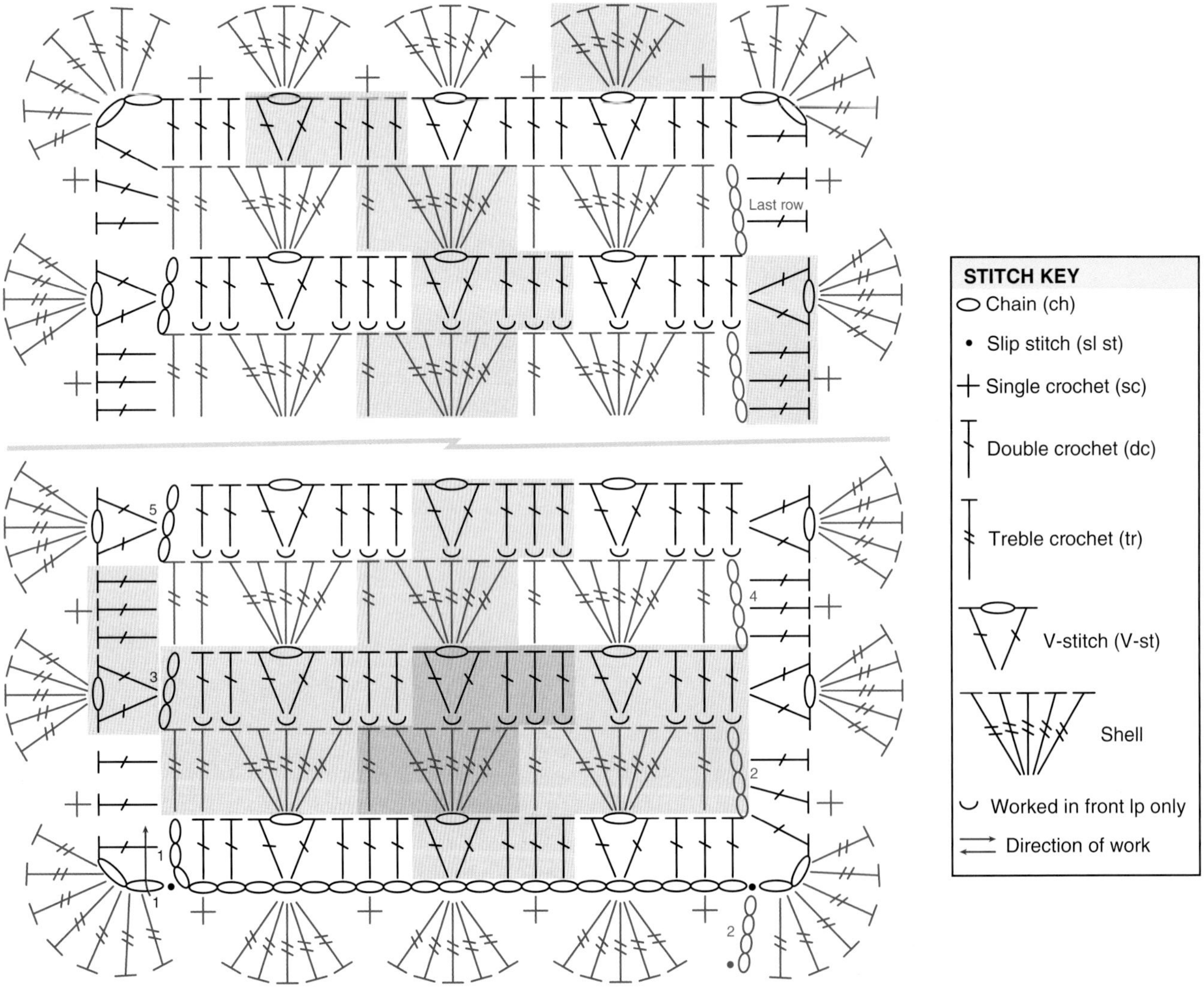

Watercolor Violets
Reduced Sample of Stitch Diagram
***Note:** Reps shown in gray.*

STITCH GUIDE

Need help? ▶ **StitchGuide.com** • ILLUSTRATED GUIDES • HOW-TO VIDEOS

STITCH ABBREVIATIONS

beg	begin/begins/beginning
bpdc	back post double crochet
bpsc	back post single crochet
bptr	back post treble crochet
CC	contrasting color
ch(s)	chain(s)
ch-	refers to chain or space previously made (i.e., ch-1 space)
ch sp(s)	chain space(s)
cl(s)	cluster(s)
cm	centimeter(s)
dc	double crochet (singular/plural)
dc dec	double crochet 2 or more stitches together, as indicated
dec	decrease/decreases/decreasing
dtr	double treble crochet
ext	extended
fpdc	front post double crochet
fpsc	front post single crochet
fptr	front post treble crochet
g	gram(s)
hdc	half double crochet
hdc dec	half double crochet 2 or more stitches together, as indicated
inc	increase/increases/increasing
lp(s)	loop(s)
MC	main color
mm	millimeter(s)
oz	ounce(s)
pc	popcorn(s)
rem	remain/remains/remaining
rep(s)	repeat(s)
rnd(s)	round(s)
RS	right side
sc	single crochet (singular/plural)
sc dec	single crochet 2 or more stitches together, as indicated
sk	skip/skipped/skipping
sl st(s)	slip stitch(es)
sp(s)	space(s)/spaced
st(s)	stitch(es)
tog	together
tr	treble crochet
trtr	triple treble
WS	wrong side
yd(s)	yard(s)
yo	yarn over

YARN CONVERSION

OUNCES TO GRAMS		GRAMS TO OUNCES	
1	28.4	25	⅞
2	56.7	40	1⅔
3	85.0	50	1¾
4	113.4	100	3½

UNITED STATES		UNITED KINGDOM
sl st (slip stitch)	=	sc (single crochet)
sc (single crochet)	=	dc (double crochet)
hdc (half double crochet)	=	htr (half treble crochet)
dc (double crochet)	=	tr (treble crochet)
tr (treble crochet)	=	dtr (double treble crochet)
dtr (double treble crochet)	=	ttr (triple treble crochet)
skip	=	miss

Reverse single crochet (reverse sc): Ch 1, sk first st, working from left to right, insert hook in next st from front to back, draw up lp on hook, yo and draw through both lps on hook.

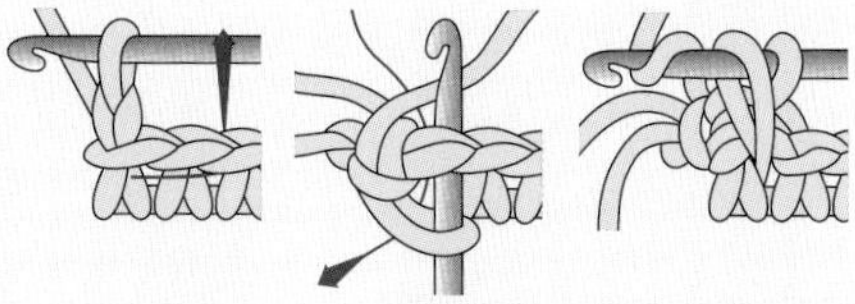

Chain (ch): Yo, pull through lp on hook.

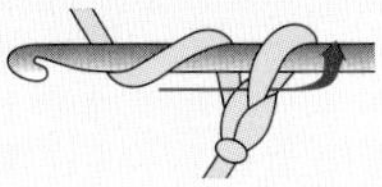

Front loop (front lp) Back loop (back lp)

Front Loop Back Loop

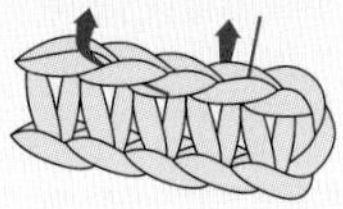

Slip stitch (sl st): Insert hook in st, pull through both lps on hook.

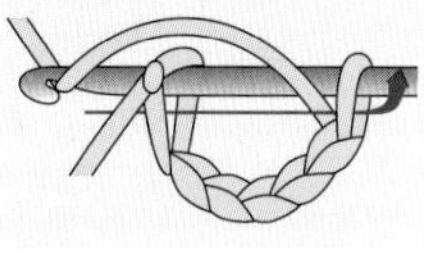

Single crochet (sc): Insert hook in st, yo, pull through st, yo, pull through both lps on hook.

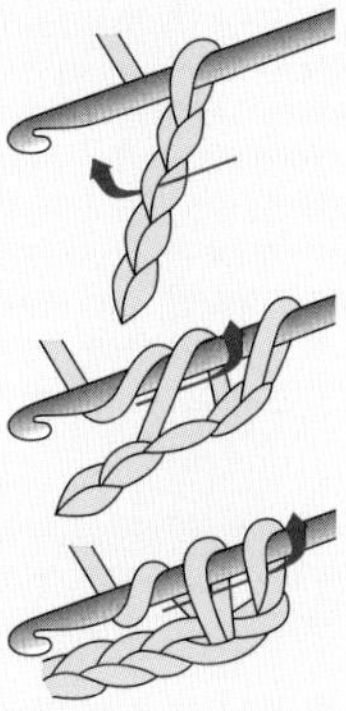

Front post stitch (fp): Back post stitch (bp): When working post st, insert hook from right to left around post of st on previous row.

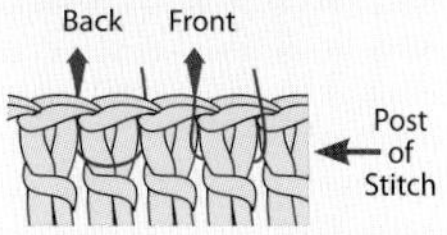

Chain color change (ch color change) Yo with new color, draw through last lp on hook.

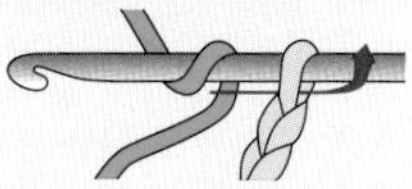

Half double crochet (hdc): Yo, insert hook in st, yo, pull through st, yo, pull through all 3 lps on hook.

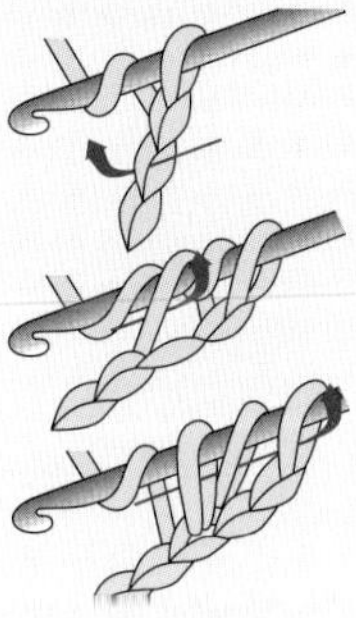

Double crochet color change (dc color change) Drop first color, yo with new color, draw through last 2 lps of st.

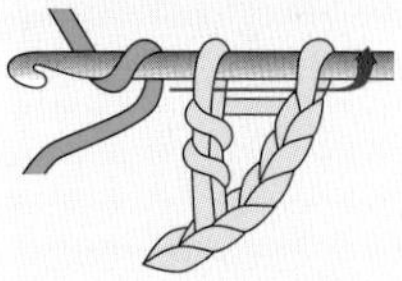

Double crochet (dc): Yo, insert hook in st, yo, pull through st, [yo, pull through 2 lps] twice.

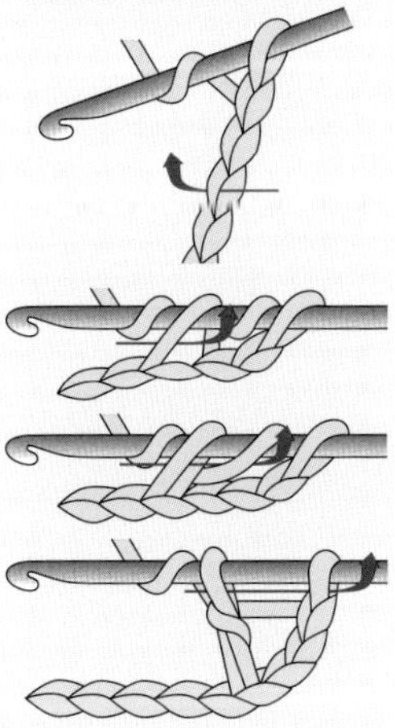

Treble crochet (tr): Yo twice, insert hook in st, yo, pull through st, [yo, pull through 2 lps] 3 times.

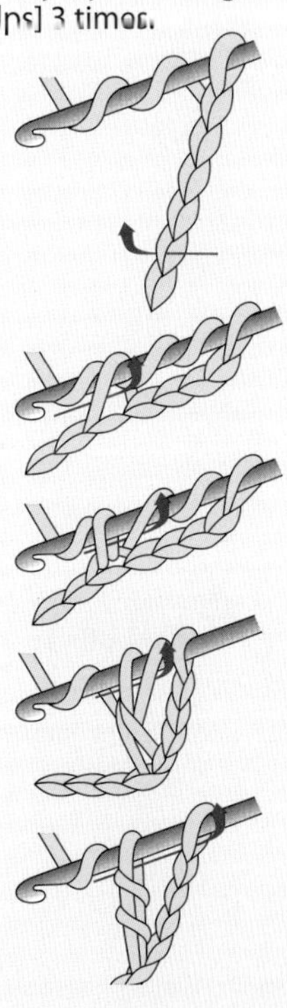

Double treble crochet (dtr): Yo 3 times, insert hook in st, yo, pull through st, [yo, pull through 2 lps] 4 times.

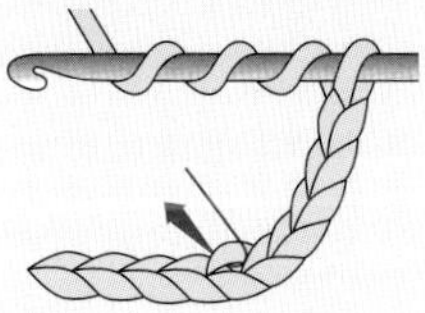

Single crochet decrease (sc dec): (Insert hook, yo, draw lp through) in each of the sts indicated, yo, draw through all lps on hook.

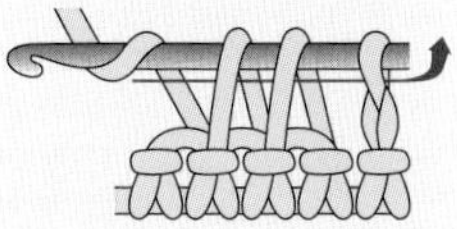

Example of 2-sc dec

Half double crochet decrease (hdc dec): (Yo, insert hook, yo, draw lp through) in each of the sts indicated, yo, draw through all lps on hook.

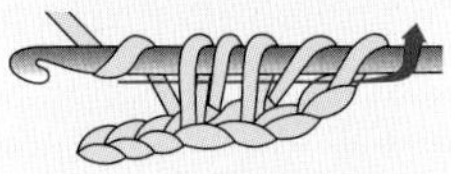

Example of 2-hdc dec

Double crochet decrease (dc dec): (Yo, insert hook, yo, draw lp through, yo, draw through 2 lps on hook) in each of the sts indicated, yo, draw through all lps on hook.

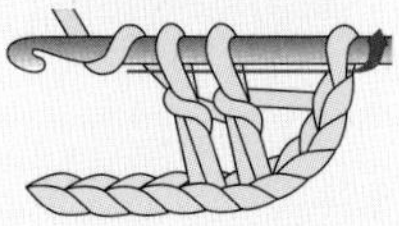

Example of 2-dc dec

Treble crochet decrease (tr dec): Holding back last lp of each st, tr in each of the sts indicated, yo, pull through all lps on hook.

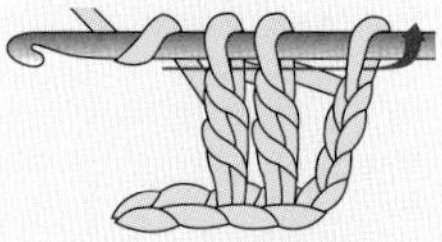

Example of 2-tr dec

Metric Conversion Charts

METRIC CONVERSIONS

yards	x	.9144	=	metres (m)
yards	x	91.44	=	centimetres (cm)
inches	x	2.54	=	centimetres (cm)
inches	x	25.40	=	millimetres (mm)
inches	x	.0254	=	metres (m)

centimetres	x	.3937	=	inches
metres	x	1.0936	=	yards

INCHES INTO MILLIMETRES & CENTIMETRES (Rounded off slightly)

inches	mm	cm	inches	cm	inches	cm	inches	cm
1/8	3	0.3	5	12.5	21	53.5	38	96.5
1/4	6	0.6	5 1/2	14	22	56	39	99
3/8	10	1	6	15	23	58.5	40	101.5
1/2	13	1.3	7	18	24	61	41	104
5/8	15	1.5	8	20.5	25	63.5	42	106.5
3/4	20	2	9	23	26	66	43	109
7/8	22	2.2	10	25.5	27	68.5	44	112
1	25	2.5	11	28	28	71	45	114.5
1 1/4	32	3.2	12	30.5	29	73.5	46	117
1 1/2	38	3.8	13	33	30	76	47	119.5
1 3/4	45	4.5	14	35.5	31	79	48	122
2	50	5	15	38	32	81.5	49	124.5
2 1/2	65	6.5	16	40.5	33	84	50	127
3	75	7.5	17	43	34	86.5		
3 1/2	90	9	18	46	35	89		
4	100	10	19	48.5	36	91.5		
4 1/2	115	11.5	20	51	37	94		

KNITTING NEEDLES CONVERSION CHART

Canada/U.S.	0	1	2	3	4	5	6	7	8	9	10	10½	11	13	15
Metric (mm)	2	2¼	2¾	3¼	3½	3¾	4	4½	5	5½	6	6½	8	9	10

CROCHET HOOKS CONVERSION CHART

Canada/U.S.	1/B	2/C	3/D	4/E	5/F	6/G	8/H	9/I	10/J	10½/K	N
Metric (mm)	2.25	2.75	3.25	3.5	3.75	4.25	5	5.5	6	6.5	9.0

Annie's®

In a Weekend: Lap Throws for the Family is published by Annie's, 306 East Parr Road, Berne, IN 46711. Printed in USA.

ISBN: 978-1-59012-237-2

1 2 3 4 5 6 7 8 9